The Art and Politics of Edward Bond

American University Studies

Series IV
English Language and Literature

Vol. 50

PETER LANG
New York · Bern · Frankfurt am Main · Paris

Lou Lappin

The Art and Politics of Edward Bond

PETER LANG
New York · Bern · Frankfurt am Main · Paris

Library of Congress Cataloging-in-Publication Data

Lappin, Lou
   The art and politics of Edward Bond.

   (American university studies. Series IV, English language and literature ; vol. 50)
   Bibliography: p.
   1. Bond, Edward—Criticism and interpretation.
2. Artists in literature.   3. Politics in literature.
4. Social problems in literature.   I. Title.   II. Series.
PR6052.05Z76   1987   822'.914   86-20907
ISBN 0-8204-0455-1
ISSN 0741-0700

CIP-Kurztitelaufnahme der Deutschen Bibliothek

Lappin, Lou:
The art and politics of Edward Bond / Lou Lappin.
— New York ; Bern ; Frankfurt am Main : Lang, 1987.
   (American university studies : Ser. 4, English
language and literature ; Vol. 50)

ISBN 0-8204-0455-1
NE: American university studies / 04

Cover photo: Edward Bond.
Courtesy of Chris Davies and Methuen, Inc.

© Peter Lang Publishing, Inc., New York 1987

All rights reserved.
Reprint or reproduction, even partially, in all forms such as microfilm, xerography, microfiche, microcard, offset strictly prohibited.

Printed by Weihert-Druck GmbH, Darmstadt (West Germany)

I would like to dedicate this book to my parents, whose encouragement and enthusiasm are gratefully acknowledged.

TABLE OF CONTENTS

Introduction: Politics and the Aesthetic Experience........ 1

Chapter 1. The Artist in Extremis........................ 17

Chapter 2. *Narrow Road* and the Avocation of the Artist.... 29

Chapter 3. *Bingo*: The Life of Shakespeare................ 47

Chapter 4. *The Fool*: The Artist and Commercial Culture.... 69

Chapter 5. *The Bundle*: The Artist as Any Man.............. 91

Chapter 6. Preface to *Lear* and *The Woman*................. 109

Chapter 7. *Lear* and the Reconstruction of Tragedy......... 117

Chapter 8. *The Woman* and Sexual Politics.................. 149

Chapter 9. Conclusion..................................... 171

Bibliography 183

INTRODUCTION

The preoccupation of the English stage with politics has been explained in terms of its unique ability to display a time in which men's ideals and practice bear little relation to one another. The theatre, David Hare argues,

> ...is the best way of showing the gap between what is said and what is seen to be done, and that is why, ragged and gap-toothed as it is, it has still a far healthier potential than some of the poorer, abandoned arts.[1]

Hare's words support the cultural theory that the art of a period is organically related to its way of life and idea of community; as a result moral, aesthetic and social judgements are inevitably connected.[2] The recognition of culture as a social process and the effort towards the integration of art with the common life of society is of special significance to the contemporary English stage and most particularly, Edward Bond. The role of the artist as agent of revelation is a generally conceded cultural phenomenon. But the premise behind Bond's intellectual and imaginative work suggests a rejection of the specialization of art and a refusal to treat aesthetic issues in isolation. Instead, the power of the plays and the conviction from which Bond gathers his dramatic energy resides in the writer's vision of social organization and activity. Rather than a figure unruffled by the materialism of political and economic considerations, the artist sifts through and revalues the materials of his social experience. The tension that Bond reveals in each of his plays has remained essentially unchanged: the balance between the individual and the external world, the exploration of man in relation to his actions, especially to the extent that he is dispossessed of his own autonomy. Bond's work investigates the rationale for the gaps that occur so consipicuously to Hare, the space between what men say and what they accomplish, between their ideals and their actions.

Bond's sense of alienation and commitment to political change is bound to his working class background, the experience of World War II and an overwhelming sense of disaffection in modern capitalist society: "Why in the first place do we live in urban, crowded, regimented groups, working like machines (mostly for the benefit of other men) with no real control of our lives?"[3] His plays imply a response to fundamental issues confronting English society; not surprisingly, they are dominated by images of decline and decay. The threat of nuclear destruction and ecological disaster, the creation of mammoth bureaucracies and a competitive society in which rational political action seems impossible, are reflected in a series of plays in which madness (*Narrow Road*, *Bingo*, *The Fool*, *Lear*, *The Bundle*, *The Sea*) crystalizes a culture in crisis. Familiar categories no longer confirm the individual in a structure of values that once reassured him. Instead, the England that provided the force behind Bond's plays is presaged in political tracts entitled *Britain in Decline*, *The Strange Death of Liberal England* and *Break Up Britain*. Each in their own way formulates a rationale for social entropy, political stasis, and economic decline. For Bond, the capitalism that was resurrected because of the inability of socialism to sustain itself provides a meaningless form of aggression; technology is unable to guarantee the satisfaction of human needs or provide culture, and instead deprives people of their humanity. The dissolution of the post-war empire deprived the economy of revenue as well as diminishing England's status as a world power. The fact that England is now classified economically with Spain, Greece, and Portugal rather than with France, Germany and Japan, and the loss of face over the challenge posed by Argentina in the Falkland Islands intimate a loss of national pride. But the instability of the pound and the inflationary economy provide the severest pressure for an economic system already burdened by an unstable balance of payments:

> The Gross Product rose only eighteen points in the decade 1968-1978....Industrial productivity was even worse, remaining stagnant from 1969 to 1971 and then declining from 1973 until 1978. Unemployment rose steadily and under pressure of these economic realities the political parties lost their ideological distinctiveness.[4]

With no counter ideology, and a sense of helplessness over the absence of an alternative system that might encourage change, political legislation seems unable to sustain the depletion of energy and commitment. Certainly a portion of the disillusion, especially for those educated out of the working class, was the failure of the Labor movement to institute a productive socialism. Despite the post-war elections and the wave of nationalization and social welfare legislation that seemed to empower government with the public interest, despite the temporary expansion and prosperity of the fifties, England has been unable to overcome her economic problems. In spite of the rebirth of hope in the 1964 Labor constituency, the working class underwent no transformation. What had at least constituted a common purpose and a mutual willingness to sacrifice seemed to dissolve. Class origin continues to play an essential role in determining one's future, and upward mobility has proved difficult. In spite of efforts to redistribute the wealth through income and inheritance tax policies, a 1974 survey indicated that twenty-four percent of Britain's citizens held eighty-six percent of her wealth. Though Margaret Thatcher's Conservative leadership attempted to improve conditions by reemphasizing market incentives and encouraging private enterprise, unemployment continues to rise and inflation remains uncomfortably high. Though the policies instituted by Labor since the war are often held accountable for the declining rate of economic growth, a sense of failed purpose and public despair seem to imply a deeper malaise that impedes the nation's productivity.

The life of Edward Bond and his determination to enact a "method of change," albeit in imaginative contexts, provide a particularly passionate response in this framework. Bond's parents were farm larborers who were forced to find work in London during the depression of the thirties. Bond left a secondary school of "obedience and authority" by his own choice at fifteen, and credits a good deal of his accomplishment to that decision. But it was the experience of war and glimpses of its devastation that organized a perception of experience that has undergone little change:

> I think it was because I was brought up in a war, the moment I start sitting at my typewriter I get involved in those fundamental questions simply because I was born into a society in which you didn't know if you were going to last the day....When I was young I saw people running for their lives. So these questions come very naturally to me....I am concerned with important issues, that's part of my basic response...[5]

The experience of the evacuation politicized Bond, not so much through a particular platform or ideology but as an ontological way of grasping reality:

> The reason that I'm interested in politics is that I grew up in a political situation where everything was seen in term of politics....You were always involved in questions of necessity. Politics was the way one experienced growing up.[6]

He recalls labelling himself an "anti-conservative" at twelve, and in the 1945 Elections he recounts watching a black woman canvassing for Churchill and realizing the "class structure was vicious and dangerous."[7] After ten years of anonymous factory and office jobs, Bond entered National Service and found the army's class structure and institutionalization a process that forced him to take writing earnestly:

> What really started me writing seriously was being in the army because that presented a lot of problems that I had to sort out in some way. So that was certainly why I became the sort of dramatist I became. The army's a sort of parodied version of civil society...the naked barbarism. It's a very corrupt form of society and a very foolish and vicious form of reverence for dead idols...[8]

Part of the problem is the growing isolation and separation among men which prevents human beings from achieving their potential. Bond attributes this to a generalized lack of community responsibility--what is missing from our society. Political organization and the nature of human beings exist in conflict.

The fusion of political organization and human beings to produce culture, "what he (a person) is and what will become of him,"[9] implies for Bond the most compelling aspirations of art--the most essentially human form of appropriating reality. The figure of the artist encapsulates that possibility because art and social behavior inevitable reflect a sense of living in a specific social system. His artist figures, in every instance, create in accordance with the type of relations they have with society. Artists reflect the contemporary state of knowledge of society; society in turn defines the responsibility of the artist. So the artist cannot be indifferent to the social relations in whose framework he creates. In this context, it has been said that society gets the art it deserves. Bond's artist figures occupy a frame of reference that implies a deterministic response to material circumstances and the immediate present rather than a subjective, idealized range of experience outside history. Though my subject is not the exploration of the figure of the artist in English culture, Bond's premise suggests the rejection of the languid apostle of culture parodied in the aesthete figure of Bunthorne in Gilbert and Sullivan's *Patience* and portrayed in *Punch* in the 1870's and 1880's. The aesthete implied in Wilde's critical dialogues-- *The Decay of Lying* and *The Critic as Artist* --imply that art is more interesting than life and that the object of art is an imaginary world superior to reality; style rather than the subject determines value. Pinero's *Trelawny of the Wells* (which was designed to help implement realism) and even Shaw's artist-aesthetes profess an admiration for love, beauty and finer ideals. The image of the artist in these plays implies a self-referential figure whose aspirations are confined to a subjective, internalized process that exacts no toll on any life beyond its own, nor any response that possesses ramifications for the life of society. The life of art does not serve to challenge or question the values of a social structure which accepts and defines the artist as a figure who inhabits a mysterious and solipsistic field of perception. This mutual acceptance on the part of society and the artist (in literature) implies a rigid social hierarchy in which each comfortably knows his place. However, the figures of Bond and the work of Griffiths, Arden and D'Arcy, Barker, and Osborne imply an important shift in the relation of art to life--from a self-reflexive subjectivity to an impasse where the vocation of creative activity is coterminous with failure, madness, and the renunciation of society all together. The artist figure in these plays no longer functions as a bestower of arcane value or a purveyor of rarefied experience. Instead, they live lives of social necessity; and their consistent frustration and denial suggest the contingencies of experience in the latter half of the twentieth century. In these plays, the work of art, or the presence of the artist, is insufficient to assure a human society. The reconquest of the world can't be accomplished by art alone. In plays like *The Entertainer*, *Teeth N'Smiles*, *The Island of the Mighty*, *Comedians*, and *No End of Blame*, experience is validated by rational encounter, by making sense of the permutations of the political and social order rather than through abstract or idealized gestures.

The life of art implies for Bond, and for his contemporaries, the foundation of human freedom because the idea of creativity is deeply implicated in what Bond has defined as the moral imagination. "All imagination is political,"[10] Bond argues, and the feeling is shared by his contemporaries, whose artist figures are beset by dilemmas whose origin lies outside art and in the laws of capitalist material production. In each play, the anatomization of the creative process reveals a growing constriction and a sense of entrapment when the artist can no longer satisfy a human need for fulfillment in the objective world. The plays represent a search for a form to express such a refusal. When art ceases to respond to internal needs and only satisfies the demands imposed by society, creative freedom is destroyed. The exteriorization and separation between art and the human need to conceive and create are the climactic events in the life of the post-Shavian artist. Creative activity in these plays implies a process of self-consciousness; as the action unfolds, it bears witness to its protagonists' refusal to integrate themselves in a society with which they have ceased to identify. But the price is devastating. The subsequent loss of liberty and spontaneity comes to imply not only the loss of creative powers, but the loss of faith in all men's freedom. Archie Rice's "deadness behind the eyes" formulates a metaphor for his estrangement from society. Dependence on drugs and alcohol anesthetizes Maggie in David Hare's *Teeth N' Smiles*, while the white heat of Gethin Price's frustration isolates him from the rest of the comics in *Comedians*. Isolation, solipsism, and the inability to communicate culminate in madness, ironically the apotheosis of creative energy with no means to objectify itself in the experiential world, for Clare, Shakespeare, Merlin (*Island of the Mighty*) and Bela (*No End of Blame*).

For Bond, alienation and the form it takes in civil society possess particular interest. Marx's theory of spiritual dispossession and creative depletion, of psychic energy annulled, deferred and isolated by a set of social and economic laws might serve as metaphor for the dilemmas of Bond's artist figures. In a generalized way, the process of alienation provides an image for the life of all Bond's characters. His theory of art requires that every man be creative and cultivate his moral imagination. One critic explains all Bond's plays, not simply the ones that implicate writers and poets, as concerned with the denial of the imagination. Marx's theory provides a general model for the dispossession and alienation of the imagination. Erich Fromm provides a definition[11] derived from Marx that is particularly useful while George Lukács poses Marx's ideas in more explicitly dramatic terms:

> This is the dramatic conflict: man as merely the intersection point of great forces, and his deeds not even his own. Instead something independent of him mixes in, a hostile system which he senses as forever indifferent to him, thus shattering his will. And the why of his acts is likewise never wholly his own....Men are but pawns, their will is but their possible moves, and it is what remains forever alien to them (the *abstractum*) which moves them.[12]

The core of Marx's writing about alienation was conceived in an early work, *The Economic and Philosophical Manuscripts of 1844*. The publication of the *Manuscripts* in 1932 revealed an aspect of Marx that had been relatively undetected: the humanist who was aroused by issues of man's self-realization. The context of his argument derives from the decline of feudalism and the growth of capitalism at the end of the Middle Ages. Under capitalism, the worker does not own the means of production; the product of his labor, consequently, does not belong to him, but to the owner-capitalist who consumes his powers without replenishing them:

> the worker is related to the product of his labor as to an alien object....The alienation of the worker in his product means not only that his labor becomes an object, an external existence, but that it exists outside him, independently, as something alien to him. It means that the life which he has conferred on the object confronts him as something hostile and alien.[13]

In the *Manuscripts*, Marx argues for the primacy of a humanism based on individuality and selfhood, a potentiality sustained through productive activity and generated by man's need to express and give external dimension to his psychic energy. As a "spontaneous," and "self-directed activity," labor functions as a process of self-creation in which man objectifies and experiences himself as an active, conscious figure. The objects he creates reflect his nature and permit self-evaluation. Ideally, it is a self-reflexive process in which man transforms the world to satisfy his needs and then gazes at his own reflection in the objects he has constructed. Capitalism, however, undermines this process: affirmation dissolves in denial, self-creation is displaced by dispossession, and fulfillment is dissipated in exhaustion. When man's labor is alienated, it exists independently, outside the control of its producer. Rather than fulfillment through work, labor ceases to embody the creative individual as an expression of his creative powers. As a social process, alienation formulates a civil society composed of separate selves. Identity is restricted to one's particular self; selfish needs dissolve in a world of atomistic, antagonistic individuals in a process that Marx calls separation through surrender--man is abstracted from the social whole because he has surrendered his product to the market place. Dispossessed of his relation to his creativity, he loses touch with all human specificity; little remains of his relation to his activity, product, or fellow man. Under the prerogatives of alienation, a unique configuration is transformed and the idea of class becomes predominate in social relations. Estrangement from productive activity finds its correlative in the estrangement of social relations. Dislocation and depletion exclude the idea of sociality--work no longer expresses an individual's personality and needs. Bertell Ollman summarizes this process:

> Man is spoken of as being separated from his work (he plays no part in deciding what to do or how to do it)--a break between the individual and his life activity. Man is said to be separated from his own products (he has no control over what he makes or what becomes of it afterwards)--a break between the individual and the material world. He is also said to be separated from his fellow man (class hostility has rendered most forms of cooperation impossible)--a break between man and man. In each instance, a relation that distinguishes the human species has disappeared.[14]

The creative character of labor and its indispensability in the life of man might be compared to the necessity of art in the humanizing process. Each share a creative impulse and a need for satisfaction and affirmation in the experiential world. R. Schacht comments that the "paradigm of such activity (labor) would seem to be artistic creativity."[15] Joachim Israel indicates that "the description of the function of labor to a certain extent fits the artisan's activity...the artisan's shaping every product in an individual way, making of it an expression of his personality and being attached to it..."[16] Bertell Ollman implies that Marx himself blurred the division between work, activity and creativity:

> ...there is no clear distinction in Marx's writing between activity, work and creativity. In interacting with nature each man deposits part of his personality, the distinctive contribution of his powers, in all he does...all work in any area of life...may also be viewed as creativity. Marx even speaks of a worker's productive activity as his creative power. Rather than a belittling of creativity, its equation with activity and work represents an unusual extension of these other concepts.[17]

Though Marx devised no organic theory of art, the way he relates creativity to labor provides a model to interpret the way the Bondian artist is dispossessed of his own brand of creative activity. Whether creativity is precisely equivalent to art is less consequential than that for both Marx and Bond creativity is an informing principal of human value. In the social worlds that Bond devises, the artist, like Marx's worker under capitalism, is alienated because he does not recognize himself in his product and is deprived of creative and spiritual freedom. Yet it is essentially his social relations that determine his freedom, and only through some form of revolutionary transformation is freedom possible. To this degree, Bond is certainly a Marxist; and the act of writing is an ethical activity charged with a moral imperative.

In his critique of capitalism in the "Introduction" to *The Fool*, Bond describes the inequity between the actions a society must perform to keep its social structure running and what it must do to maintain its humanity. Capitalist economy, he concludes, is dependent on exploitation and aggression: "We need anti-social behavior to keep society running, but such behavior destroys society. The worker must 'know his place' in the factory, but be an insatiable egotist outside it."[18] The lack of control over political and economic institutions demands a "method of change," a redistribution of power from the hands of the ruling class which maintains its existence through violence and organizes it politically. Bond concurs with Marx when he claims that human nature is a result of social relations: our subjective selves are created through objective social interaction--change is dependent on the alteration of our political and social base. Such reconstitution suggests the dissolution of a class society that empowers an irrational consciousness until the economic basis of society is so inconsistent with its social structure that it can no longer function. The humanistic necessity for such revolutionary change is what Bond has been groping toward from 1968 to 1978 (the parameters of this study). His plays provide the response to his own question, "Can the human species survive?"

For Bond, the connection between art and reality is a humanizing impulse that creates a self-conscious, rational society: "Art isn't about itself, it's about how men relate to the world and each other; it's not a private or even individual experience, but one of the ways society creates its identity."[19] The artist's function is to create public images in which the audience recognizes themselves and confirms their identity. Art formulates a method of self-consciousness that "places the individual in the world and interprets the world in accordance with human needs and possibilities."[20] Its purpose is not only to reveal new truths or reclaim old ones but to show how man can reshape experience from the circumstances the world provides.

Accordingly, Bond acknowledges his discomfort with absurdist writers; he cannot concede that life ultimately resolves in chaos or violence.

> Life becomes meaningless when you stop acting on the thing that concerns you most: your moral involvement in society. Indifference and cynicism, and pseudo-philosophy (we're all animals), pseudo-psychology (we're all basically selfish) and pseudo-science (we all have a need to act aggressively) add up to that pseudo-profundity: life is absurd.[21]

These are the misinterpretations imposed by the ruling class that distort the real function of art, which is "the imagination of the real," unless the writer records experience "...it doesn't become an event in history but remains inert, brutal fact."[22] Bond's art is based precisely on such a recognition; he terms it a "rational theatre" because "theatre when it's doing what it was created to do, demonstrates order in chaos, the ideal in the ordinary, history in the present, the rational in the seemingly irrational."[23] Life, Bond insists, need not be an "ungraspable flow of experience."[24] The theatre is capable of revealing the irrationality of the world and the need for justice that is not fulfilled in the social order.

While Bond's theatre suggests a guarded optimism and implies that experience is susceptible to rational analysis, his work has only partially begun to fulfill the Left's exhortation for the creation of a theatre which is interventionist on the political level. Rationality for Bond implies a purposefulness, a rational and moral engagement in the life of society that in dramatic terms implies the acquisition of some form of insight on behalf of his characters, if only an oblique recognition of the irrational society they inhabit. If social change is Bond's purpose, his art remains inseparable from his politics: "Asking artists to keep politics out of art is as sensible as asking men to keep politics out of society. Men without politics would be animals, and art without politics would be trivial."[25] It is inconceivable for Bond to contemplate an art insulated from social experience, moral responsiblity or the interests of the writer. In the "Preface" to *The Bundle*, he accepts the use of left wing political violence if it helps to create a rational society, a combative position he had earlier disavowed.

Yet Bond remains a writer in transition. From 1968 to 1978 he admits a movement from

> being intuitively political to being consciously political; from talking about social comment to talking about socialism; from talking about morality to talking about socialism; from being socially committed to being committed to a socialist society.[26]

If he had possessed a political attitude, he hadn't always the vocabulary to formulate it: "I was aware of the injustice and in that sense I had a class attitude to it...but I wasn't aware of it conceptually. I had no conceptual language to enlighten others."[27]

John McGrath, whose 7:84 Theatre Company is a Marxist theatre group designed to bring socialist theatre to the working class, has emerged as one of the most articulate spokesmen and ideologues for a theatre organised "within the shadow of the ideas of Marx."[28] McGrath's theatre is predicated on political change, the insistence that theatre, to achieve its artistic objectives, must take part in a liberating form of socialism. In the process, it disavows the bourgeois artist whose reference point is anything but the present. Like McGrath, Bond envisions a theatre that analyzes the corruption of man-made institutions and foresees the creation of socialism as instrumental for political change. McGrath's comments at a Conference on Political Theatre at Cambridge shares the exigencies of Bond's idealism and their passionate insistence for a theatre

> ...that has as its base a recognition of capitalism as an economic system which produces classes; that sees the betterment of human life for all people in the abolition of classes and capitalism; that sees this can ony happen through...the working class and through democratization--economic as well as political--of society and its decision-making processes; that sees the establishment of socialism...as another step towards the realization of the full potential

of every individual human life during the short time that every individual has to live.[29]

For Bond and McGrath, the creative recording of experience provides an element that formulates an energy discharged in revolution, an image of human nature that insists upon change.

ENDNOTES

[1] David Hare quoted in C.W.E. Bigsby, "The Language Crisis in British Theatre: The Drama of Cultural Pathology," in *Contemporary English Drama*, ed. C.W.E. Bigsby (New York: Homes and Meier, 1981), p. 41.

[2] Raymond Williams, *Culture and Society* (New York: Columbia University Press, 1983), p. 130.

[3] Edward Bond quoted in Catherine Itzin, *Stages in the Revolution* (London: Eyre Methuen, 1980), p. 81.

[4] Op. cit., No. 1, p. 50.

[5] Malcolm Hay and Philip Roberts, *Bond: A Study of His Plays* (London: Eyre Methuen, 1980), p. 22.

[6] Tony Coult, *The Plays of Edward Bond* (London: Eyre Methuen, 1977), p. 10.

[7] Ibid., p. 10.

[8] Op. cit., No. 5, p. 15.

[9] Edward Bond. Introduction," *The Fool* (Chicago: The Dramatic Publishing Co., 1978), p. xiii.

[10] Edward Bond, "Introduction," in *Bingo and the Sea* (New York: Hill and Wang, 1975), p. xi.

[11] Erich Fromm, *The Sane Society* (New York: Holt and Rinehart, 1955), p. 56. By alienation is meant a mode of experience in which the person experiences himself as alien. He has become, one might say, estranged from himself. He does not experience himself as the center of the world, as the creator of his own acts--but his acts and their consequences have become his masters....The alienated person is out of touch with himself as he is out of touch with any other person. He, like the others, is experienced as things are experienced...but at the same time without being related to himself and to the world outside productively.

[12] George Lukács, "The Sociology of Modern Drama," trans. Lee Baxandall in *The Theory of the Modern Stage*, ed. Eric Bentley (Baltimore: Penguin Books, 1960), p. 430.

[13] Karl Marx, *The Economic and Philosophic Manuscripts of 1844*, ed. Dirk Struik, trans. Martin Milligan (New York: International Publishers, 1964), p. 108.

[14] Bertell Ollman, *Alienation: Marx's Conception of Man in Capitalist Society* (Cambridge: Cambridge University Press, 1976), pp. 133-134.

[15] Richard Schacht, *Alienation* (Garden City, New York: Doubleday, 1970), p. 80.

[16] Joachim Israel, *Alienation: From Marx to Modern Sociology* (Boston: Allyn and Bacon, 1971), p. 39.

[17] Op. cit., No. 14, pp. 101-102.

[18] Op. cit., No. 9. p. xvi.

[19] Malcolm Hay and Philip Roberts, *Edward Bond: A Companion to His Plays* (London: Eyre Methuen, 1978), p. 67.

[20] Op. cit., No. 9, p. xvii.

[21] Edward Bond, "Author's Program Note on *The Sea*," in *Bingo and the Sea*, p. 124.

[22] Edward Bond, "Introduction: The Rational Theatre," *Plays: Two* (London: Eyre Methuen, 1978), p. xvi.

[23] Ibid, p. xiv.

[24] Edward Bond, "Preface," *The Bundle* (London: Eyre Methuen, 1978), p. xvi.

[25] Op. cit., No. 19, p. 69.

[26] Op. cit., No. 3, pp. 76-77.

[27] Ibid., p. 79.

[28] Ibid., p. x.

[29] Ibid., p. x.

Chapter 1

THE ARTIST IN EXTREMIS

In calling attention to artist types and reflecting on writers in particular, Bond has dramatized certain myths that the ruling class uses to maintain its ascendency and to show how human nature and culture are formed:

> ...one of the reasons why two of my plays have dealt with writers as major figures is simply because they can be clearly seen to be caught up in this process. What I have done is try to find representative figures from the past...to see how they were functioning as writers....I don't think there is a special problem for the writer anymore than for a dentist or bricklayer. What my plays with authors deal with is the problem of what is culture...what I want to say is unless you have something called culture as opposed to simple organization then the issue is not that a writer will be locked up, but that you will have H-bombs like those ten miles up the road from here.[1]

Bond implies, as others have before him, that the treatment of artists and artistic experience provide a standard for the health of a civilization--the standards of society in part lies in the existence of the conditions of the artist's activity and purpose.[2] Though Marx never developed an integrated cultural or artistic theory, he indicates in the "Preface" to his *Critique of Political Economy* that

> the mode of production in material life determines the general character of the social, political and spiritual processes of life. It is not the consciousness of men that determines their existence but, on the contrary, their social existence determines their consciousness.[3]

Accordingly, Bond's advice to actors playing his characters is applicable to his artist principles: define yourselves "in relation to other characters...consider the nature of the action rather than the nature of the self."[4] For Clare, Basho, Lear, and Shakespeare, the subtext of motivation has been displaced by the necessity to comprehend the political and economic laws that bind society. The shape of a drama in which the idea of character and political and economic necessity intersect is an aspect of George Lukác's argument "that the drama of individualism (and historicism) is as well as the drama of milieu."[5] Bond's characters are precisely a product of this tension. Though his central characters initiate and determine the course of the action, and the plays, at least on one level, are called into being for the sake of a single character's spiritual success or failure, the issues Bond raises are informed less by single acts of self-determination than by the larger focus of history. Though heroic acts remain possible and indeed occur, Bond's characters occupy a dramatic universe in which personal fate is subsumed by the more urgent task of testing whether the political and economic laws of community are viable. Though Bond's figures possess their own generative power, they remain fated by an abstract necessity (usually of social and economic origin) that directs their destiny.

The plays demonstrate how such a necessity is historical and problematic; Bond creates contradictions between the artist and a society whose values he does not identify with. In Bond's social orders, existence is quantified and abstract; the artist and society remain opposed. Art represents (for Clare, Lear and Shakespeare) denied humanity and opposes an inhuman society; and society opposes the artist as he resists, and tries to express his humanness. Without being conscious of it, the artist opposes society by remaining faithful to his creative will; he is unwilling to integrate his thought and work in an alienated community. At his most heroic, he resists an inert universe; he refuses to exalt an inhuman reality and searches for a form to express his denial. Bond defines such a dilemma at least partially in class terms:

> Whatever the social origin of the artist, his point of view is always decided by the ruling class. The ruling class have the surplus value to create art or to have it created for them—their influence is predominate. They control the normative values of society by legal and economic control of the mechanical functioning of society.⁶

Part of the effectiveness of the plays is that despite their creative impulses, Bond's artists can never escape the hard edge of their practical reality or the necessity of their social selves. Rather, they inhabit a framework of moral possibility, like the rest of society, in which they are faced with choices which either confirm their humanity or deny the impulse to be rational. Bond never attempts to explain or demystify the idea of creativity, but instead measures their achievement ironically, through a personal growth of moral sanity. In many ways, they possess a common range of human failings that are no different from any other socially based individaul. So it is especially hard to comprehend Albert Hunt's logic that Bond has failed to attract an audience because of his "increasing self-indulgence as a writer in what he himself calls a writer's theatre."⁷ Hunt assumes that Bond ascribes a privileged status to the writer's profession, a mystical truth which Bond mistakenly associates with an elitist tendency to venerate artists. Bond has given "free rein to his obsession" and in the process, Hunt claims, has become "trapped by his own literary aspirations and...lost touch with the society he is trying to explain."⁸ But to imply that the dilemmas of Lear, Basho, Hecuba, Clare or Shakespeare bear no relation to the lives of anyone but other artists, is to misunderstand Bond's strategy. The suggestion that his characters remain separate and distinct from life, and that the social experience of the artist quantitatively varies with every member of society, is a misreading of the plays. Rather than cut off from experience, Bond's artist types are made or broken by their encounters with social reality; art is prescribed by the political occasion in which it is created. The creative lives of Clare, Shakespeare, Basho and Lear, if anything, are diminished in the social experience of the plays. Our experience of these figures lies not so much in their imaginative powers as in the way social experience is organized around their failures. We may not possess the ability of a Shakespeare or a John Clare, but to reconstitute society we do not need to. Art is imagined through the experience of history; and Bond derives his dramatic energy from testing the gap between the individual's art and his personal experience. In a world where it is not always possible to be human, Bond challenges the prerogative of the artist to act rationally and creatively in his personal life.

The affirmation of the interdependence of art and the political event in which it is contained is part of a tradition in which William Morris linked the "cause of art...[and] the cause of the people."[9] It is a tradition which includes Oscar Wilde's admission, albeit in a paradoxical framework, that "an artist is not an isolated fact, he is the resultant of a certain milieu and a certain entourage."[10] Though his dramaturgy diverges considerably, he approximates, Katherine Worth notes, "the moralist playwrights in the Shavian tradition, to Osborne and even Shaw himself."[11] He certainly shares with Shaw a preoccupation with unjust social structures as well as Osborne's capacity for representing pain, suffering and the inertness behind Archie Rice's eyes. Yet Bond is the product of an age in which, the historian R.E. Warner maintains, capitalism has little use for culture:

> The progress of culture is dependent on the progress for the material conditions for culture; and in particular, the social organization of any period of history limits the cultural possibilities of that period...social organization can and does lag behind what from the point of view of culture is both possible and desirable.[12]

Bond's political idealism combines a humanistic socialism and a belief in the vitality of a theatre to provide a self-reflexive image of man in society. Theatre, Bond insists, possesses the potential to affect and alter the way people interpret and understand themselves. His role in the theatre is explicitly related to his socialism, which supplies the basis for his interpretation of the artist (even if it is occasionally overstated):

> The writer must not be a cult figure or genius or any nonsense like that. He's just a member of the working staff of the theatre....I'm just a member of the theatre like, for instance, the man who does the lights....There is no mystique about it. There is only a simple factual expertise of learning your job.[13]

The purposefulness of Bond's plays, the function of the artist, and the responsibility of all rational people converge in the objective of the writer, whether they are figures in Bond's plays or individuals who reside in contemporary society:

> ...the job of rational people, of writers, of dramatists is to plead for a just society, to state clearly the conditions under which we live and try to make everybody understand that they must bear the consequences for the sort of life they lead. To show that our society is irrational and therefore dangerous--and that it maintains itself by denigrating and corrupting human beings.[14]

Socialism furnishes the means to implement responsiblity and liberty, the creation of a classless society and the destruction of an anachronistic social structure. Bond perhaps speaks for a generation of young British playwrights as well as for a generation that has more kinship with John Osborne when he declares

> all the justifying mythology of the past is no longer operative for most people. People no longer believe that the Queen is particularly good for us, or that people who happen to be born in big houses should be called Lords and in some curious way should have political wisdom....That sort of world view has come crashing down. All of that world view was a mythology which enabled a certain class structure, a certain economic organization to exist. The structure is gone, what we have now is an irresponsible society which does not teach people any genuine responsibility for each other.[15]

Though art alone can't formulate a moral society, it's a necessary part of its creation; its interpretation of experience--a warning about the danger society is in--logically culminates in the creation of culture: "...the rational creation of human nature, the implementation of rationality in all human activity, economic, political, social, public and private."[16] The creation of culture plays an essential part in Bond's humanism and provides the locus for the symbolic relationship between art, rationality and imagination. The production of culture is the nexus where the artist is endowed with substantive fulfillment in relation to society. It is the argument of the plays that the artist and private individual possess the potential to regulate its growth when their beliefs are in accordance with the way they experience their lives. Artists should be purveyors of culture, but in the context of the plays they are forced to make choices for culture or the perpetuation of a false system of values. Only by comprehending political necessity, as Shakespeare and Basho cannot, as Lear and Hecuba barely accomplish, can artists sustain culture. The decision-making process of these figures enables the audience to grasp the pressures that political compromise exerts as well as the consequences of human action.

Though Shakespeare, Lear, Basho, and John Clare all end their lives tragically in a conventional sense, there remains something curative about their deaths that is life-affirming. Tragedy supplies us with

> ...something to use in our lives, that gives us sympathy and understanding of other people. Tragedy in this sense is necessary for moral maturity, it doesn't lead to despair, and it certainly has nothing to do with a catharsis that makes us accept abominations to which there should be political solutions. It leads to knowledge and action.[17]

The lives of Shakespeare, Lear, and Clare are all designed to conclude with a new set of creative possibilities for action. In one sense, their failures are so insistent not because they are artists, but because something in them has failed that is common to all of us. Each of us, Bond contends, possesses a moral imagination--a means of perception that is no longer the prerogative of an artist figure but is instrumental for anyone interested in assuring his own moral sanity. To measure the conventional success of one of

Bond's characters is less important than our collective realization that we as audience members possess in some degree that capacity for imagination. If all imagination is political, as Bond argues, then creative imagination remains necessary to culture; "without it we are denatured animals....A society that excluded the criticial part of itself."[18] Such imagination is based on a moral/politicized vision of reality that orients our experience of the world. While Bond's artists possess the maximum potential for inculcating creative imagination, moral neutrality or pursuit of personal illusions endangers the health of society. In this sense, all Bond's plays are about the imagination and its repudiation. The inability of his characters to apprehend and evolve their humanity is finally a failure of the imagination. The absence of commitment leaves no ground for moral values to operate and issues in confusion, physical depletion, and a sense of radical insufficiency. Tony Coult tells us that

> Imagination is our most essentially human faculty, because it allows us to predict the results of our actions, to see the connection between cause and effect. It thus has a vital moral dimension. A sense of responsibility is the result of a cultivated imagination, and a society which devalues the imagination, or which allows it to develop in children in the wrong way, will have a greatly diminished sense of morality.[19]

In the process of the plays, Bond's artists perform a psychic balancing act between their social persona, society, and their imaginative capacity. Clare's poems, Shakespeare's plays and Lear's destruction of the wall are creative acts that challenge the irrationality of the world. In *Lear*, *The Woman*, *Bingo*, *The Fool*, *Narrow Road to the Deep North*, and *The Bundle*, the absence of culture militates against the creative imagination and the impulse to humanize the environment; the capacity to measure and imagine the feelings and sufferings of others has been eroded by political institutions and social regulation. In a culture where obsessions with aggression, competition, and the ethic of individualism and self-sufficiency are operative, it is not surprising that the extinction of the creative imagination results in the dissolution of human values. Bond's artists are formulated expressly to clarify this dilemma. As Bond says of Shakespeare, "One can't have a beautiful soul that floats free of one's involvement in the world."[20]

Bond places his artist figure in the same contradiction or dilemma in each play; he is caught in the polarity between acceptance and action. He is presented with a choice, and when this is presented to the audience, the artist becomes a potential model for action, a demonstration of "order in chaos, the ideal in the ordinary, history in the present, the rational in the seemingly irrational."[21] Bond's artists are usually entrapped by half the dialectic--they suffer from partialness, a half-formed consciousness of events. Though they don't always act in accordance with their perceptions and only subliminally acknowledge the necessity of culture, Shakespeare, Clare, Hecuba, and Lear finally come to concede the efficacy of the moral imagination. But by then their fates and society's are determined. The two Bashos provide the antithesis to this vision; the first (*Narrow Road*) in his ironic posturing and the second (*The Bundle*) in the way he incarnates sinister self-interest. In one way, each of Bond's figures refuses to acknowledge fully his human nature. If art is the individual claiming a rational relationship with the world, Bond's artists are all failures. They learn they can't escape their social selves (a process that Bond the artist acknowledges simply by writing plays) yet, Bond argues, the fault is not their own. Each comes into contact with a culture and social structure that enervates them. (Bond's work has seen few productions in his native country.) Capitalism for Clare represents a meaningless aggression that explicity interferes with his creative process. Shakespeare is seduced by the measure of security that the vested interests provide, and Lear's monarchy constitutes an equally aggressive regime before he is deposed. In each instance, society does not permit the artist to exist in the way they evolved. Seen this way, the artist's purpose is to mediate the relation between the present and its idealized vision. It can never commit itself to pessimism or despair.

It is a short step to conclude, as Bond does, that the artist's existence implies the uneven development of art and society. Bond's artists emerge as figures of frustration and denial because they are in part historically conditioned by an ideological structure that determines the extent of their creativity, but perhaps more significantly, order their personal values and psychic well-being. Because of the class origins of the artist, whether he is upwardly mobile like the Bashos of *Narrow Road* and *The Bundle*, achieved bourgeois respectability like Shakespeare, falls back to his working class roots as John Clare does, or witnesses his kingship (*Lear*) overthrown, the ideological character of art functions as an expression of social division, and implies movement up or down the social and economic scale. The figures of Bond's artists reflects this paradox of dependence and creativity. Raymond Williams sorts out the dilemma of such figures:

> As creators of consciousness they help determine social reality. As figures dependent on political and economic structures they operate to reflect this structure and its reality as well. They provide a crucial link in hindering or changing it.[22]

Bond's artists can't renounce their personal freedom without sacrificing their artistic activity. They can't cease to create to escape the conflict; they can't choose a life of silence without destroying the process that entitles them to their identity. Though the artist remains a symbol of the development of human consciousness and possesses the foundation of human freedom, the life of art or of moral imagination isolates its visionaries from the social continuum. Bond demonstrates the sterility of these individual struggles when they are undirected or express little awareness of the roots of alienation in the political and social structure. When they are somehow implicated in the structure of the ruling class as the Bashos, Shakespeare, and Lear appear to be, they make abstractions out of their real existence and sacrifice their individuality to the formality of bureaucreatic functionalism and brutality. Though his characters are shaped by the environments they inhabit, they resist facile typing; instead, they are carefully determined by their familial, social and economic relationships. While Bond examines the dialectics of social reality, his characters focus on the "pursuit of illusions--of false solutions to personal and political problems."[23] Bond notes, "I show characters in their various social roles and various social relationships (and thus achieving wholeness) rather than developing characters from a geist."[24] Yet despite his insistence on rationality, there is something poetic and emotive in the plays, an aspect of resonancy and ambiguity in which, according to one critic, "inner changes occur which don't have reverberations in the political sphere."[25] At its best, it is a drama of personality made conscious. Katherine Worth acutely notes that Bond "creates an extraordinary sense of characters who are at some deep level wishing to be wrenched out of their habitual ways and thrust into a perception they have hitherto avoided."[26] Bond's characters crystalize precisely at those moments when the central character pauses to reflect and ask the question is change necessary? His plays recreate the contradictions that provide the antagonisms and the polarized confrontations that initiate awareness. "If you follow the development of the plays," he comments, "you will see the typical twentieth-century man, worried about society and searching for some way to live personally....The plays are an examination of what it means to be living at this time."[27]

ENDNOTES

[1] Hay and Roberts, p. 181.

[2] I owe many of my perceptions about the relations of the artist and society to Adolpho Vasquez, *The Artist and Society* (New York: Monthly Review Press, 1973).

[3] Karl Marx, "Preface," to *Critique of Political Economy* quoted in *Culture and Society*, p. 266.

[4] Edward Bond, "On Brecht: A Letter to Peter Holland," *Theatre Quarterly*, 8, No. 30 (1978), p. 35.

[5] Lukács, p. 434.

[6] Op. cit., No. 20, p. xiii.

[7] Albert Hunt, "A Writer's Theatre," *New Society*, 11, December 1975, p. 607.

[8] Ibid, p. 607.

[9] William Morris quoted in *Culture and Society* (New York: Columbia University Press, 1983), p. 154.

[10] Oscar Wilde quoted in *Culture and Society*, p. 170.

[11] Katherine Worth, *Revolutions in Modern English Drama* (London: G. Bell and Sons, 1972), p. 171.

[12] R.E. Warner quoted in *Culture and Society*, p. 270.

[13] K.H. Stoll, "Interview with Edward Bond and Arnold Wesler," *Twentieth Century Literature*, 22 (1976), p. 420.

[14] Op. cit., No. 13, p. 418.

[15] Beverly Matherne and Salvatore Maiorana, "Interview with Edward Bond," *Kansas Quarterly*, 12, IV, pp. 66-67.

[16] Op. cit., No. 9, p. xi.

[17] Edward Bond, "Author's Program Note on The Sea," in *Bingo and the Sea*, p. 124.

[18] Op. cit., No. 9, p. xv.

[19] Coult, p. 71.

[20] Daniel Jones, "Edward Bond's Rational Theatre," *Theatre Journal*, 32 (December 1980), p. 510.

[21] Op. cit., No. 20, p. xiii.

[22] *Culture and Society*, p. 249.

[23] *Companion*, p. 56.

[24] Op. cit., No. 32, p. 34.

[25] Katherine Worth, "Edward Bond," In *Essays on Contemporary British Dramatists*, eds. Hedwig Back and Albert Wertheim (Munich: Hueber, 1981), p. 208.

[26] Ibid., p. 205.

[27] Donald Hall, "Interview with Edward Bond," *The Guardian*, 29 (September 1971), p. 10.

Chapter 2

NARROW ROAD AND THE AVOCATION OF THE ARTIST

When he wrote *The Narrow Road to the Deep North* in 1968, Bond had only partially formulated the artist persona of his later plays. The idea for the play originated in an account of *The Records of a Weather Exposed Skeleton* by a Japanese poet, Matsuo Basho. When he discovered the story of a poet who refuses to help an abandoned infant and instead pursues the path to "enlightenment" Bond admits, "I thought that was absolutely what a poet should not do. He should have picked up the child. That was the responsibility of poetry."[1]

Though composed out of his indignation over a single incident, the play is subtitled *A Comedy*, and the figure of Basho is drawn broadly enough to encompass a series of parodic impulses. At the same time, Basho is the source that Bond uses to demonstrate historical process: the way a social organization is held together by the aggression it creates.

> ...as far as I am concerned, if Basho is going to function like a man, like a human being, he picks that child up, he does not leave it there abandoned. What I say is that if society is based on that sort of disregard for fundamental, I think, human instincts, then I think that society must end up in some sort of disaster.[2]

Basho's decision initiates a historical process that implicates the two other sources of moral influence in the play--Shogo and Georgina. His moral choice radiates outward into the life of the community and intersects the development of all the major characters to demonstrate that "aggression has become moralized and morality has become a form of violence"[3] in the politics of the play. Whether Basho functions as an ironic commentator, a comic foil, a contrast to Bond's own point of view, or a sphere of influence in his own right, his movement and development in the life of his culture prophesy the dissolution of community.[4]

From the outset, Basho's self-conscious address to the audience in the "Prologue" is informed by a pretention that undermines the speaker's authority: "I am as you know, the great seventeenth century poet who brought the haiku verse form to perfection and gave it greater range and depth."[5] The recitation of the poem, however, provides the audience an opportunity to consider the poet before we evaluate the man. The "flawless" haiku reveals the superficiality of Basho's art--"Silent old pool/ Frog jumps/ Kdang" (p. 7) is a parodic distortion Bond derived from the original: "Breaking the silence/Of an ancient pond/ A frog jumped into the water/ A deep resonance."[6]

As Basho anticipates his journey for enlightenment, he begins to resemble a cartoon figure framed by a fairytale mission rather than a poet whose intention is to comprehend the finiteness of human destiny. When he discovers an abandoned infant on the river bank he utters with childlike simplicity, "Why did its parents do that?" and implicitly resists involvement. In his first encounter with the world he responds by musing on the circumstantial facticity of the event rather than its causes or implications. Despite the plea of the parents, "We're poor and there's no food...if we let this one go perhaps the others will live" (p. 8), Basho rationalizes his uneasiness by philosophizing: "It hasn't done anything to earn this suffering--it's caused by something greater and more massive, you could call it the irresistible will of Heaven. So it must cry to Heaven, and I must go to the North" (p. 8). Basho's response to the infant signifies his removal from the social process and human-centered values. The quest for enlightenment takes the form of a self-aggrandizing principle that is a means to gratify the ego's need to objectify itself in quasi-metaphysical gestures of spiritual and artistic purity.

Jane Howell, who directed the play's first production, attributes Basho's responses to its generic source--the artistic impulse:

> I think Basho's reactions are perfectly consistent. For me he is a petty representative--God forgive the word--artist. In the pursuit of the perfection of our craft, we attempt to retain the center of ourselves in order to create, at the cost of not committing ourselves to the world, not noticing the world as it really is.[7]

The concept of enlightenment and the isolation of a hermit is an abstraction designed to contrast with the material circumstances of the infant. What is perhaps more important, as Tony Coult suggests, is that Basho "locates the centre of his being outside himself...whereas for Bond the protection of life is an absolutely fundamental instinct rooted in human identity."[8] Through the "Prologue," Bond reveals the contradiction that exists to some extent in all his artist figures, though in this instance Basho's insensitivity is almost comically distorted. Bond's figures occupy a paradoxical framework in which life and art, deed and thought, and action and spirit are divided. It is a gap that never occurs to Basho, that Shakespeare consciously overlooks, that Clare attempts to mediate, and the Basho II figure of *The Bundle* attempts to suppress. Yet Shakespeare and Clare are at least conscious of their own deficiencies. Basho II's specious reasoning and narcissistic self-absorption are conditions that Clare, Shakespeare and Lear come to comprehend whether they act on their conclusions or not. Yet Bond does not provide Basho I with similar insight; his arguments are not derived from any compelling dramatic source but are founded on his insistence on hyperbole and detachment. Basho's avocation is merely a means to addresss his social behavior:

> What particularly incensed me about Basho was that everybody says, oh, what a marvelous poet. I think that is absolutely phoney. I mean that is bad poetry, that's academic phoney poetry, all the things he said. But I am really talking about his actions.[9]

Bond is explicit in explaining that he is not so much interested in exploring the possibilities of creativity as searching for a means to address the inequity between an individual's actions and his belief. He found it particularly convenient to adopt a prototype whose identity has been historically split by the dichotomy of action and thought. In *Narrow Road to the Deep North*, the artist and society exist apart; the artist resembles a comic persona sanctified by a mission that is founded on a vague religiosity designed not to protect life but to gratify its own needs. Basho's mission is ratified by the irresistible "will of heaven," an idea held up to as much ridicule as its emissary.

Bond's objective in this early play is to demonstrate that Western society has provided the individual with no viable political system. The burden of proof lies in the series of moral choices that present themselves to Basho. Thirty years later, he tends to speak in terms of abstractions and non-human concerns. His quest has been reduced to a descriptive catalogue of his travels; the young pedagogue has become an old pedagogue. Enlightenment, he sagely acknowledges to a potential disciple, may be obtained by standing twenty-nine and a half years facing a wall: "I saw there was nothing in the Deep North that I'd already known everything before I went" (p. 10). Bond observes that

> Basho says, for instance, that you get enlightenment where you are and so on, and everybody says, oh how profound. People like Basho never get enlightenment where they are because, you know, enlightenment should have come in the first scene...where he found the child.[10]

Basho's sophistic reasoning establishes that enlightenment remains elusive; his words confirm his preoccupation with pseudo-abstraction and uninterest in finite social relations. But his speech remains ambiguous enough to suggest the half wisdom rooted in cliché. Bond argues that Basho fails to connect his quest for knowledge with any application to human forms because he does not really quest: "...what the play reveals is that the knowledge and meaning he talks about are meaningless. How do you know it? Look at the way he behaves--his political action."[11] Basho's obsessiveness with form is further revealed when he tests a young supplicant's faith by demanding that he describe the physical appearance of god. When Kiro, the naive but sincere initiate, describes the deity in human terms--a figure with two hands, two eyes, two lips--Basho admonishes, "You don't know anything about god, you've only been looking at men" (p. 8). God represents the unknowable, an other worldliness that bears little relation to the world of men. Accordingly, Basho presumes that enlightenment endows him with the prerogative of policy making; abstraction supercedes human needs and activity. It is a logic designed to impede human contact, to find vindication in forms and finally capitalizes on the poet's instinct for the maintenance of his own superiority. Basho's denial of social reality at the behest of artificial institutions prevents him from creating human culture.

After two years of wandering, Basho's only response to the fascist regime that indiscriminately executes dissidents is speculation on the status of his orchard and the complaint that relatives of the condemned run about "looking for somewhere to cry." Basho's response is to move his hut. His gesture implies that life resists human intervention and represents god's intentionality. Even as the dictator's soldiers drag him away, he meticulously dictates a poem to a nun--its factuality and central image recreates his own powerlessness and formalizes his indifference:

>   The old horse stops on the bridge
>   The carter unhitches and leads her from the shafts
>   Legs broken
>   Passers-by help to push her in the river
>   Head down, mane in eyes
>   The carter goes off between the shafts.
>   (p. 13)

In an image that resonates with the earlier sacrifice of the infant--the passiveness of the carter and horse, the ineffectual struggle, the capitulation of the passers-by, and the final indifference imply a philosophy of acceptance and self-preservation; anything that cannot be altered is passively endorsed. Basho's concern that Shogo pursues him because "He knows I've got enlightenment and he doesn't like people knowing something he doesn't," (p. 13) typifies his belief that enlightenment, rather than possessing any spiritual utility, is a trophy of material value, a mark of distinction which entitles him to rank and privilege.

On the way to the dictator, Basho reencounters the young novitiate, who has an ancient pot caught on his head. Though gasping for breath, Basho refuses to aid the young priest because the relic is "sacred and old." He ridicules Kiro for not possessing sufficient knowledge or enlightenment to escape its weight and comically advises "think small." The suggestion defines Basho's comic essence as well as his philosophy. Yet he displays a certain shrewdness when he takes Kiro along to test the tyrant's wisdom.

Shogo is the second center of meaning and creator of culture we encounter. A tyrant who usurped power, his city inflicts a relentless and authoritarian social order for the "common good" of the people. Since society prevents man from total regression and violence, the ruthless enforcement of Shogo's policies is designed to "prevent suffering" and "stop the chaos," but is actually legalized murder. Shogo admits to Kiro, "...life makes people unhappy...People are born in the tiger's mouth. I snatch them out and some of them get caught in the teeth" (p. 39). Shogo's fascism, Bond implies, is the result of an abandoned infant (we subsequently learn it was Shogo whom Basho had left by the river) who grew up mutilated. A victim of a political system that demands aggression, Shogo symbolizes how, in Tony Coult's words, "Human beings are forced to respond to whatever their society presents them with and it is these moments of choice, to accept the status quo or not, that are symbolized by Basho's actions."[12] In Bond's dialectical development of history, Basho's disregard for the infant predetermined and formulated the shape of Shogo's city-state.

When Basho is finally brought before Shogo, he can only utter with solemnity, "You can kill me, of course, but it will have no importance" (p. 23). The comic absurdity of his indifference to the destruction of his own life and his subsequent refusal to look after the former emperor's children because he is unwed parody his obsession with form. But when Shogo destroys the pot on Kiro's head, Basho is ironically politicized. Confronted with the violence and fascism of Shogo's regime, he sputters with rage, but for the wrong reasons:

> He's imprisoned innocent women, orphaned children, made the men soldiers, and killed them. His city is hell, ruled by atrocity. I could put up with that if I could still hope. But how can I hope if he destroys religion? He knew the pot was sacred. Of course, that's only a symbol, but we need symbols to protect us from ourselves. If he destroys them, there's no future. A fool destroys men but a fanatic destroys their hope. (p. 27)

Politicized by his own brand of religiosity, Basho helps to enforce and preserve the myths of the dominant political institutions. His sensibility is elaborated in the philosophy of Combe in *Bingo* and Milton in *The Fool*. Each insists that man defer to abstract symbols of power and convention, an obligation to conformity that sustains the status quo. The destruction of a thousand-year-old pot impels Basho to take action and provides Bond with the means to dramatize the irrationality of society. Even Basho's engagement in life, even his belated activism provides Bond with a comic impulse. After he considers the merits of bribery and poison as political tools, Basho pauses to reflect on the course of events and admits somewhat petulantly, "I don't like meddling in politics, like most people. I have more important things to do.

But if politicians can't solve this problem, someone must" (p. 28).

In the first four scenes of *Narrow Road*, Basho functions as a comic purveyor of enlightenment. His rationale barely conceals his own inadequacy, self-interest, and the spirit of the "learned pedagogue" or self-important provincial artist. As an audience, we tend to overlook or simply dismiss his actions because of their transparency. By the end of four scenes, Bond begins to reveal the consequences of his acts; the result of detaching himself from the mainstream of social relations and his concern with the abstraction of form. We discover that in all probability, Shogo was left behind on the river bank and that his subsequent experience of the world had formulated his personality:

> What I am saying is that if the child does survive...it will have been taught that the world in which it finds itself is not an uncomfortable world, but an absolute alien world that it must fight....Human beings are produced into, are told that their environment is their enemy. They must fight it all the while. So, of course human beings become vicious, wild, dangerous, and the rest of it...you could say Basho didn't save the child so the child grew up dead.[13]

Though he is instrumental in teaching Shogo his first lesson about life, Basho is never held culpable for his acts, nor does he bear the burden of blame in the action of the play. Rather, he remains an outsider, never comfortably integrated in the play's social hierarchy. Bond comments that he "turned Basho into a sort of hollow zombie. One of those people who appear immensely cultured, with all the filigree of culture, all the outward show, but as hollow as can be."[14] Basho functions more as a structural vehicle for Bond to disperse a series of concepts upon without having to bear the dramatic consequences. Part intriguer, a parody of the artistic temperament, and a means to polarize all of Bond's discontents, he possesses a cartoon-like flexibility rather than the complex motives of Bond's more mature figures. The question of guilt or innocence in a fragmented capitalist society never arises because

Bond's dramatic method has not yet created the complex social matrix against which Clare, Shakespeare, Basho (*The Bundle*) and Lear find themselves pitched. *Narrow Road to the Deep North* functions more on the level of bitter parable in which the characters' gestures and actions imply allegory. The disparity between what Basho says and what he desires--enlightenment and isolation in his garden and politicization in spite of himself--provides Bond with the comic and ironic texture of the play. Basho's gradual ascent to power is dictated less by principle and more by his inability to suppress his outraged sense of etiquette. His political involvement results in the exchange of one repressive regime for another. What there is of his art resides in an impure aestheticism separated from the world of events. If events do not implicate him personally, temporal politics do not seem worth his attention; his response is justified by the way events treat him. Since Bond has not yet considered the dilemma of the creative temperament, Basho resembles an opportunist who insinuates himself into the ruling class to consolidate his own interests.

Yet Basho possesses a number of vital impulses, including the ability to survive; he neither goes mad like Georgina or is subject to the horrible disembowelment Shogo undergoes, the other centers of "value" in the play. Instead, Basho displays a resilience that sometimes impedes Bond's own assessment of him:

> ...perhaps I ought to have said in my introduction 'The villain in this piece is Basho!' But I think that's a bit unfair to him, because I think if one tried to understand him a bit more, then one would have to extend one's sympathy to him, too. But from the political viewpoint...there is no ambivalence...at all.[15]

Bond himself seems divided between the figure who represents the amorality and self-serving instincts of a false culture and his own impulses to create a character that resists facile reduction. Though conventionally unscrupulous,

Basho I is not the crafty representative of capitalism that Basho II of *The Bundle* becomes, nor does he possess the ruthless power over life and death that Shogo wields. By his first action, he renounces society and political responsibility, but he is portrayed so naively that his gradual appropriation of power is barely noticeable. When threatened with death, he clings to a philosophy divested of commitment and remains confident in his superiority: "I'm going to die. No one can open and shut the door at the same time" (pp. 23-24).

Though his artistic qualifications exist only nominally, and Basho is incapable of creating the culture that implies moral responsibility, Bond has begun, if obliquely, to consider the way the artist relates to his community. Despite his disregard for human values, Basho inadvertently manages to affect the life of society more than Clare or Shakespeare; if nothing else, his life reflects the irrationality of society. In a dramatic causality that seems to function through a series of loosely connected events rather than careful dramatic plotting, Basho's indifference shapes the life of the community and creates the government over which he will ultimately preside. The relations between artist and society is determined by the quality of Basho's sensibility, even if it is a broader and less defined relation than Bond creates in subsequent plays. The structure of society remains primitive and dependent on the will and moral policy of its three major characters rather than the consequence of a complex economic system. Yet the play remains Bond's first indication of the effect an artist type can have on the life of the community.

Political pressure and personal impulse merge in Basho's second foray to the Deep North. The expedition is a quest for power "five times more ruthless" than Shogo's and results in the transformation of Basho into a "man of action." When Basho appeals to Georgina, the third center of human consciousness in the play, he readily accepts "soldiers and guns to kill [his] enemies" for an evangelical "love of Jesus." Like Basho, Georgina uses tradition and iconography, symbols that emphasize the efficacy of form, to enable her to "protect" the people. When he admits to Georgina that the people seem more content under her rule, she disagrees. Instead of Shogo's "rule by atrocity" she employs moral inhibition:

> I persuade people in their hearts that they are sin and have evil thoughts, and that they're greedy and violent and destructive, and---more than anything else--that their bodies must be hidden, and that sex is...corrupting....When they believe all that they do what they're told. They don't judge you--they feel guilty themselves and accept that you have the right to judge them....If sin didn't exist it would be necessary to invent it. (p. 42)

The poet priest who quested for thirty years in search of enlightenment finds it convenient to align himself with Georgina and so becomes a purveyor of Christianity. Moreover, he and Georgina embody the conservative forces of order and tradition that resist progress and restrict the evolution of culture. At the same time, he is an innocent foil for the Commodore and Georgina's dreams of empire. Bond portrays him as a naive idealist and uncharacteristically innocent as he formulates doubts about the new regime:

> BASHO. D'you mean you weren't...sincere?
> GEORGINA. (laughs) Did you think I was?
> BASHO. Yes....I admired you for it.
> GEORGINA. Why?
> BASHO. Well, you don't use the sack
> GEORGINA. Oh, there'll be a few hangings.
> BASHO. But the people will be happier.
> GEORGINA. Of course they're not! (pp. 41-42)

As Basho comprehends that Georgina relies on the corruption of men's minds to control them--"We need the devil to protect people from themselves" (p. 42)--he speaks prophetically: "People who raise ghosts become haunted" (p. 42). Though his sudden regard for the welfare of the people is not quite prepared for, his vocation as an artist permits Bond to use Basho's words as a measured response to the various levels of moral experience he encounters.

Basho functions in a way that Clare, Shakespeare or Lear cannot because of their self-conscious individuality. Basho's very peripheralness and lack of commitment provides the audience with a detached observer. He is a choric observer who provides an attitude about the relations between government and the society it presides over. He remains a mediating presence whose comments are directed at the audience's understanding of the events and an ironist who views Georgina and the Commodore, spectres of British imperialism, as a lesser evil. It is through his eyes that the demogoguery and tactics of nascent capitalism are most clearly drawn, but the process complicates our perceptions of Basho. As an artist, his poems and philosophy are of minimal interest; as a prophet of enlightenment, we view him with repugnance, but we share his point of view as a naive observer who, like much of the audience, may be politically ingenuous.

After an insurgency and counter insurgency, Shogo's forces are defeated and the new regime enlists Basho's service as a puppet governor. In the climactic scene of the play, Kiro, alone and disconsolate, reads Basho's poems while Basho presides over an investigation of Shogo's regime. As Kiro examines the poems, Basho's voice pontificates offstage in a public apologia and explanation of the most recent coup. Bond counterpoints the voice of the artist (Basho the "poet") and the voice of government (Basho the "prime minister") simultaneously. One mourns the sterility of the natural order in lyric terms and by implication the life of the city--"A feather falls from the sky/ There are no birds here/ The nests are broken/ The migration's over/ The soil was dry" (p. 55)--while the other, as various critics have pointed out (see Scharine, Durbach and Tener), "rationalizes the failure of moral action which has precipitated this condition."[16]

> ...I, Basho, saw the child, I saw it in its rags by the river, already lying in its own filth. I looked at it and went on. Oh god forgive me! If I had looked in its eyes I would have seen the devil, and I would have...held it under with these poet's hands....I am a poet and I should have known. (p. 56)

Not only has Bond literalized Basho's complicity and shrewdness (he has assimilated much from his experience with Shogo and Georgina), he also demonstrates how the voice of the poet, despite its aspirations to wisdom also claims a stake in the savagery he laments. By ironically contrasting the two voices, Bond reveals the potential of the artist and how that power is misused. Though it is perhaps too simplistic to assume that Basho might have reconstituted the history of the city if he had provided a single child with human kindness, it is that sort of action that at least provides the impetus for the growth of culture. The poems are ultimately a reinterpretation of Basho's vision of the world; he is a false prophet who inadvertently transforms political reality to harmonize with images of his own sterile sensibility. Finally, the ego protects itself by asking for forgiveness rather than assuming responsibility.

This last scene summarizes the way Basho's art remains separate from life. At every opportunity, Basho resists ethical choice, and persists as a comic persona in a self-destructive world. By the end of the play, Basho hardly resembles a harmless idealist sequestered in an ivory tower. By acquiring power he encourages a cycle of imperialism and subjugation--"false culture." By acting in the interest of authority and organized religion, by mastering all the correct slogans, he comes to embody the dominant institutions.

Basho is incapable of providing an image of human culture partially because Bond, the dramatist, has not yet clarified the full measure of his artistic persona. Instead, he has devised an image of the artist as a "hollow zombie" that provides the play with its comic irony and makes certain that more complex issues do not arise. Basho is so self-centered that we barely consider his ability to formulate culture. In the future, Bond will use the image of the artist to demonstrate the working out of the rational laws of society, but Basho is so undifferentiated and flatly conceived as an artist (though not as a dramatic character) that any process he undergoes remains circumscribed by his personal limitations. His lack of commitment in his art is reflected metaphorically when Shogo casts aside a sheaf of his poems. As the poems are casually tossed away, Basho remarks absent-mindedly, "It's of no importance, I have copies. But we won't leave them here, it looks unsightly" (p. 53). Shogo disdains Basho's poems as empty gestures that have no bearing on his life. The pages flutter through the air and settle aimlessly. Basho responds to Shogo's gesture in the way he responds to most things in the play--formally, as the circumstances dictate. As the scene unfolds, the idea of collecting useless poems is extended. As Basho chronicles the political realities of the investigation, the audience listens to images from his art. As he utters his last words: "Shogo is dead. The sin is broke. Let the new city live forever" (p. 57), Kiro begins a ritual that will conclude with his suicide. Kiro's self-embowelment and his disregard for the shouts of a drowning swimmer provides a final reflection on Basho's art, his public policy, and the cycle he has initiated. Kiro's last words--"I drain the cup/ At the bottom/ Flags" (p. 56)--is a poem of Basho's that emblemizes the substance of his artistry, an art of appearance that venerates symbols but resists human contact. Basho, Georgina and Shogo are all bound by their willingness to sacrifice what is instinctive and human--culture, in the the name of abstract principle. Richard Scharine tells us that "Basho sacrifices humanity in the name of heaven, Shogo sacrifices humanity for the sake of the city. Georgina would teach humanity to sacrifice itself in the name of heaven and for the sake of the city."[17] However, Basho provides the impetus for the action of the play, and it is his art and philosophy that ignores the potential for renewing society.

The play's last image rests with Kiro and the futility he experiences. The single figure who seemed capable of altering himself is disaffected by experience. Gentle and contemplative, and a more likely prototype of the artist's sensibility, Kiro has been the only seeker of knowledge in the play. Yet his very inactivity has condemned him; his detachment had infuriated Shogo--"You don't live, you sit and play with yourself and think of god" (p. 46)--are words that also might be used to condemn Basho. The last scene unfolds as he ignores the swimmer's cry for help and recreates Basho's gesture of disavowal at the beginning of the play. It is this skepticism that is Basho's legacy--an inability to constructively affect the world he inhabits: "Kiro, with all his introspective enlightenment...and understanding...puts himself in the same position as Basho," suggests Bond, "because he doesn't understand or cannot accept the necessity of social action."[18] Whether he is too self-absorbed to respond to the needs of the drowning figure, or whether he is a failed moralist whose inactivity signifies the futility of living in the world, he is implicated by Basho's sphere of influence.

In *Narrow Road* Bond explicitly demonstrates the potential of moral choice and the consequences of the renunciation of that responsibility. Bond dreamily rhapsodizes, "In an ideal society he (Basho) would have picked the baby up, gone off the stage and there would have been no necessity for a play."[19] Unfortunately, the historical process initiated by Basho's first action is extended as he proclaims, "Let the city live forever." The proclamation must be regarded sardonically, with portentous irony. The sentiments reflect the capitulation of a petty ego that luxuriates in the idea of self-imposed exile yet is equally comfortable in a position of public leadership and responsibility. Each mode of action is undertaken for the sake of the "ideal" in whose name it will sacrifice people. This disconnection between the search for meaning and its correlative in human beings creates the gap between the individual and the community.

ENDNOTES

[1] Glen Loney, "An Interview with Edward Bond," *Performing Arts Journal*, 1, No. 2 (1976), p. 48.

[2] Irving Wardle, "A Discussion with Edward Bond," *Gambit*, 5, No. 17 (1970), p. 9.

[3] Edward Bond, "Author's Preface," *Lear* (New York: Hill and Wang, 1972), p. vii.

[4] Adolph Barth, "The Agressive 'Theatrum Mundi' of Edward Bond: *Narrow Road to the Deep North*," *Modern Drama* 18, No. 2 1975), p. 7.

[5] Edward Bond, *Narrow Road to the Deep North* (London: Eyre Methuen, 1968), p. 7

[6] Matsuso Basho, *The Narrow Road to the Deep North and Other Travel Sketches*, trans. N. Yuasa (Harmonsworth: Penguin, 1966).

[7] Peter Ansorge, "Director in Interview: Jane Howell," *Plays and Players*, 16, No. 1 (1968), p. 70.

[8] Coult, p. 24.

[9] Wardle, p. 9.

[10] Ibid.

[11] Op. cit., No. 1, p. 43.

[12] Op. cit., No. 8, p. 29.

[13] Op. cit., No. 9, p. 11.

[14] Op. cit., No. 1, p. 43.

[15] Op. cit., No. 9, p. 9.

[16] Errol Durbach, "Herod in the Welfare State: *Kindermord* in the Plays of Edward Bond," *Educational Theatre Journal*, 27, No. 4, 1975, p. 486.

[17] Richard Scharine, *The Plays of Edward Bond* (Lewisburg: Bucknell University Press, 1976), p. 135.

[18] Hay and Roberts, p. 98.

[19] Op. cit., No. 9, p. 9.

Chapter 3

BINGO: THE LIFE OF SHAKESPEARE

In *Bingo*, Bond does not claim to reveal any new dramatic truths. The play, he explains, reveals

> what everone knows about the way our wishes and intentions are turned awry...[it] is about the compromises WS makes. But what right has he to call on the poor to make these compromises....Even if he shows...restraint he still has to make compromises with his own humanity.[1]

At the end of his career, Shakespeare is unable to achieve the peace that a life of self-reflection provides; instead, the opposite is true--he is restive and uneasy. Through the life of art, Bond implies, the artist reproduces his own moral sanity. In *King Lear*, for instance, Shakespeare "insisted on certain moral insights, certain priorities of conduct and you did those things even if it meant your death....Shakespeare must have known that, otherwise he couldn't have written the play."[2] However, the figure Bond creates in *Bingo* is incapable of mediating the fictive world of his plays and the actual circumstances of his life. The tension in the play inheres in the dialectic between an art which is spontaneous and humanitarian and personal experience which denies those impulses. Shakespeare, late in life and living in retirement, is not alienated from the moral propositions of his art; but he is unable to act in accordance with them. Ethical decision-making is possible only through creative artifice. The disjunction between what is possible in art and what is practical in life provides the axis on which the play rests.

Art, for Bond, provides a means of self-conscious affirmation--the satisfaction of a need to humanize all the artist comes in touch with. Creativity is a dynamic relation between the artist, his consciousness and the world. As the artist confronts reality, he endows it with human significance. While Shakespeare's interior world has been transformed by the power of his expressiveness, he has failed to transform himself. Through artifice he has created a moral imperative that has determined his relationship with the world; a process of self-creation designed to satisfy his own moral needs. But Shakespeare no longer articulates those powers, and he can no longer integrate himself in the material circumstances of Stratford. Unable to humanize or restore the inequities that occur around him, he remains incapable of treating his family with tenderness, combatting the material acquisitiveness of Combe, or feeling anything but pity for the displaced working class.

In the society of Stratford, having and using constitute his relations with the world. Consequently, Shakespeare has altered his essence; political expediency and material circumstances direct his behavior. The result of such separation implies exhaustion and loss. Though art should function as the most effective medium between the artist and the world, Shakespeare has lost touch with human specificity. The more he acknowledges the disparity between his art and his actions, the more he grasps his own impoverishment. Estranged from his creative powers, and guiltily recoiling from other men, he denies the spirit of his artistic achievement.

Bond's achievement in the play does not arise from the revelation of any particular psychology, or the perception of man's behavior in an irrational universe. Instead, he assumes if you are unjust "it doesn't matter how cultured...how civilized...how capable of producing wonderful...characters..[you are], you will still destroy yourself."[3] Since the ethical world of the plays assert themselves as reflections of the artist's personality, they stand as an implicit indictment of his public gestures. Paradoxically, Shakespeare is separated from his own art. What he comes to realize is that he has surrendered their substantive life at the cost of his own well-being; as symbolic extensions of his own powers they are lost to him.

At the beginning of the play, Shakespeare is divided, at once the creator of the canon and the landed proprietor of New Place--a private moralist and a public materialist. The two roles are split between authentic creation and false needs. Shakespeare, vaguely conscious of his own internal division, experiences life as fragmented. As a principal landowner, he is influenced too readily by the laws of the marketplace. His alienation is an economic process that is inculcated through a system of false needs; membership in the landed gentry creates false allegiances. His disaffection is signified by his loss of connectedness with the moral truth of the plays and subsequently with the formal life of art. The renunciation of such truths reflects the surrender of the artistic process itself.

Yet Shakespeare's ability to perceive reality with moral clarity remains undiminished. Instead of taking action, he aestheticizes reality--the artistic impulse remains intact but is cut off from its moral center, divested of commitment and application. It formulates itself in epiphanic and half-illuminated utterances of bear baiting, gliding swans and clean white snow. The power of expressiveness remains, but is stripped of its moral imagination. What persists are glimmerings of creativity, recalibrated fragments of the plays, broken shards of his own mental life. The concretize the gap between the "cultural hero" and the figure who signs the new poor laws to ensure his material well-being. The attempt to aestheticize reality in images, or in stylized formal address (primarily to Judith) reflects the artist's attempt to come to terms with his own disaffection, perhaps to overcome his dilemma by assimilating it artistically; in the process, the idea of writing and creativity ceases to reflect a productive and integral activity.

The inability to act has it correlative in the way the artist perceives the act of writing: "Fat white fingers excreting dirty black ink. Smudges, shadows. Shit. Silence."[4] Only by creating a humanized reality through practical measure can he lead a moral life. Yet silence and detachment have undermined his artistic credentials. Shakespeare retreats into a sphere of egoism and withdraws into the solipsistic self. He is isolated from the community, preoccupied by his private interests and haunted by images that signify his failure to act. In other men, he sees the limitation of his own freedom; his self-division reflects his separation from human values and the sacrifice of his most essential nature.

Bond argues that the root of his alienation lies outside his own persona and is embedded in the imposition of artificial needs that provide the basis for his social and economic relations. In order to promote change, one must reorder the structure of the socio-economic system. By using a figure of Shakespeare's stature as a symbol of culture, Bond demonstrates the working out of the rationality of society:

> You can't change the world by just being rational or create moral sanity by writing about it....Society has to bear the consequences for what it is. If you want to avoid these consequences the only way you can do it is not by applying a remedy on top, but by altering the nature of the problem below. So it seems to me that *Bingo* is a demonstration of the working out of certain truths about society which are rational and coherent and from which society can learn.[5]

Despite his authority, Bond concludes, Shakespeare "is still subject to the same laws as you and I or the man who drives the bus."[6] The paradox is that Shakespeare is tied to the limitations of a class system while his art is not. He is tied to Combe's economics, yet he is socially and culturally bound to a class that doesn't share the same material relations. If the material world of the artist is devalued, the creativity of the artist is also undermined;

the aesthetic cannot be divested of its social relation. If it is, the artist is split by the world he intends to create for.

As the influence of capitalism gains ascendency in *Bingo*, life becomes increasingly impersonalized and reified--Shakespeare ceases to identify with those values; he refuses to exalt an inhuman reality, but he has no form to acknowledge his refusal. As Bond admits in notes to the play, "Not a criticism of WS, because there is no alternative for him other than hanging or beheading..."[7]

Bond's interest in the play lies in the disruption of the relationship between the artist and the commmunity, in the tension between the function of art and the role of the artist. Society resists the artist as long as he tries to express his humanness. In seeking morality in his art, Shakespeare has resisted reification. In this context one might ask whether he is a victim or victimizer. Is he denied his powers of expressiveness by an inhuman society or do his gestures simply refract its insensitivity? It is clear that bourgeois society resists the artist as long as he tries to express himself. No longer actively creative, the problem becomes not how to create but how to resist, how to affirm his presence in an inhuman world. By disavowing responsiblity, by resigning himself to passive acceptance, he helps to create a society that is antithetical to artistic activity. Bond's recreation of the artist's disillusion and his rootlessness in a hostile world treats Shakespeare as if he possessed the sensibility of modern man. Rather than a criticism of Shakespeare, Bond condemns that portion of contemporary culture that denies that art has practical consequences: "Cultural appreciation ignores this and is no more relevant than a game of bingo and less honest."[8] The fact that *Bingo* and *The Fool* are called scenes of something indicate

> ...that it would be wrong to say that our problem is such and such now because of something that happened in the past. Our problem is created all the time, constantly recreated. And it's because we don't interfere with the recreations of our problems that we can't solve our problems.⁹

Bond's early stage directions indicate the tone of the play and implicitly suggest the course of its principal figure. Shakespeare nods silently, reads, and in four different stage directions "doesn't react;" he initiates no dialogue. The intimation of stasis established in the first scene is formally resolved near the end of the play when Shakespeare mournfully queries, "How long have I been dead?" In between, he recants a life divested of meaningful action and purposeful energy:

> I spent so much of my youth, my best energy for this: New Place. Somewhere to be sane in. It was all a mistake. There's a taste of bitterness in my mouth....I could have done so much. Absurd. Absurd. I howled when they suffered, but they were whipped so that I could be free....I was a hangman's assistant....God made the elements but we inflict them on each other (p. 48).

Self-imposed silence implies unresolved tension. As his daughter, Judith, paradoxically comments, reflection is insufficient: "People in this town aren't so easily impressed....We can all sit and think" (p. 18). Shakespeare remains either cordoned off from feeling or numbed from too much of it. Yet his first words belie his apparent detachment; he offers an itinerant beggar woman money. That Shakespeare is capable of a solicitous gesture is crucial to Bond's argument and is suggested in the subtitle of the play, *Scenes of Money and Death*. The subtitle suggests the primacy of nascent capitalism, and obliquely implies that Shakespeare's gesture has neither bearing on the woman's well-being nor requires any sacrifice on his behalf. Money in capitalist society destroys "human values because the consumer demand can't grow fast enough to maintain profits and full employment while human values are effective."¹⁰ Instead of ridding itself of poverty, a consumer society depends on its members as avaricious, aggressively competitive, and self-divisive. Indeed, the antecedents of our contemporary culture originate in Shakespeare's social order. In each, the acquisition of capital shapes and formulates the conventions of human behavior.

> We live in a closed society where you need money to live. We have no natural rights, only rights protected by money....Money has its own conventions and laws and when you live by money you live by these. To get money you must behave like money. When livelihood and human dignity depend on money, human values are replaced by money values.[11]

Shakespeare's avoidance of conflict at the outset of the play and his decision to evade human contact reflect a social structure in which human values are replaced by financial ones. When Combe, the principal landowner and magistrate arrives, Shakespeare fails to intercede for the beggar. His only relation to her is guaranteed by money. Similarly, he takes no initiative against Combe for the enclosure of the common fields that will destroy the rural community. In the process of the play he learns that single gestures--isolated moments of charity--have no bearing on the life of the community.

When he does speak, Shakespeare's first words betray his weariness and fatigue--"I get tired," "I don't know anything," "there's plenty of time" and prepare us for his complicity with Combe. A commercial culture, Bond explains, destroys "our moral sensitivity because the struggle for profit is much more corroding than the struggle for survival in the old pre-civilized world.'[12] Perhaps Shakespeare's need for security is not quite dramatically convincing. Yet Bond is not concerned with Shakespeare's psychological motivation: "What are his motives for withdrawing? I don't know....He's old, he's tired, he wants security....I'm not really interested in his motives."[13]

The idea of art and money (security) finally merge when Shakespeare, portrayed as an aging but prosperous burgher describes his finances: "The rents. I bought my share years ago out of money I made by writing" (p. 5). Despite the dispossession of the poor as well as the renters who don't have leases, he collaborates with Combe to guarantee his tithe income. "You'll get increased profits," Shakespeare tells Combe, "you can afford to guarantee me against loss. I invested a lot of money" (p. 6). Shakespeare refuses to commit his political authority and reveals his self-interest when he claims neutrality: "I'm protecting my own interests. Not supporting you or fighting the town....I want security. I can't provide for the future....My father went bankrupt when he was old. Too easy going" (p. 7). Such specious reasoning would be less transparent and more agreeable if this were not the figure whose plays display a

> ...need for sanity and its political expression: justice. How did he live? His behavior as a property owner made him closer to Goneril and Lear. He supported the Goneril society with its prisons, workhouses whippings, starvings, mutilations...[14]

Interestingly, Shakespeare's preeminence and moral force resides in his significance as a landowner with vested interests rather than in any artistic accomplishment. By accepting his arrangement with Combe, his complicity in the enforcement of those relationships is assured. By signing what amounts to the new poor laws, Shakespeare no longer functions as a symbol of culture or possesses a rational relationship with his society. By tacitly accepting Combe's plea--"Be noncommital or say you think nothing will come of it. Stay in your garden" (p. 6)--he enmeshes himself in a system where capital is deployed to maintain consumption and increase profits and industrial activity. Greater unemployment and higher food prices result from the loss of corn as a marketable crop as well as increased competition and aggressiveness. If the politics of fascism and brutality are recreated today, it is the function of the play to suggest the necessity for change:

> I think the contradictions of Shakespeare's life are similar to the contradiction in us. He was a corrupt seer and we are a barbarous civilization....Because of that our society could destroy itself. We believe in certain values but our society only works by destroying them so that our lives are a denial of our hopes. That makes

our world hateful and often it makes our species hateful to us.[15]

The process of the play reveals Shakespeare's self-loathing. It is a process of demythification which reveals how any man's moral life becomes lost. Shakespeare is revealed as a petit bourgeois who aligns himself with a brutal regime that is directed to the subjugation of the rural and lower class community--his compromises betray an entire class. In various instances, he consigns the Young Woman, the Son, the Old Man and the Old Woman to a life of confinement. If a rational culture, Bond contends, is based on a classless society, "the job of writers is to...argue for a just society, to state clearly the conditions under which we live and try to make everybody understand that they must bear the consequences of the life they lead."[16] The opposite position is held by the Chief Magistrate, who fatalistically insists that the only way men have discovered of running the world is "the long view": "Men are donkeys and they need carrots and sticks. All the other ways: they come down to bigger sticks" (p. 6). It is a ruthless judgment based on class antagonism; the kind of power politics that Shakespeare finds himself entangled in when the Young Woman is denied his charity because, "The law says it's an offense to give alms without a license" (p. 17). Casual insensitivity and a society depleted of human value is concealed by rhetoric, slogans of personal responsibility, paying one's debt, and the necessity of protecting the public. "That's why," Bond asserts, "law and order societies are morally resonsible for the terrorism they provoke."[17]

Shakespeare's silent complicity parallels his betrayal of the town. His inability to act undermines his instinctive good will. Ultimately, he rejects culture by avoiding the action that implements rationality. Shakespeare simply watches with discomfort as the girl's persecution unfolds. The Son envisions a form of his own Puritan extremism; Judith naively projects her own dissatisfaction with her father; the Old Man lurches merrily around the grounds revelling in his debauchment of the Young Woman. Each "theatrically" confronts Shakespeare, but this is not a performance and they are not actors. They are victims in a scenario that a play might redress through the transforming power of art. Shakespeare painfully bears witness to the meagerness of their positions, yet says nothing. Despite his silence, the mind of the artist is alive, conscious and perceptive. When the Young Woman is mercilessly seized, he sighs. His final offer of mediation is brushed aside, yet his instinctive impulses are too easily overcome. He chooses to remain, as Combe had urged, in the quiet of his garden. As the scene closes, the Old Woman portentously chastises the Old Man: "Mr. Shakespeare won't like you cryin' in his garden" (p. 19).

Alone, ensconced in silence, his language is stripped to practical, monosyllabic prose. There is no need for a more complex syntax because Shakespeare has nothing more complicated to say. His attempts to communicate with Judith are sheer formality: declarative, factual and insensate. Yet she is not without our sympathy. She pleads with her father, "people have feelings. They suffer. Life almost breaks them" (p. 18). It is part of the generalized disaffection that all the characters endure. His ailing wife, Judith tells him, stays in bed: "She doesn't know who she is, or what she is supposed to do, or who she married. She's bewildered like so many of us" (p. 18). When Shakespeare contemptuously replies, "You speak so badly. Such banalities, so stale and ugly" (p. 18), it is the form rather than her sentiments that he coldly reproves. He is not impervious to feeling, but he has organized his field of perception by detaching himself from experience and by aestheticizing reality. His criticism almost appears to be levelled against her means of expression, as if she were uttering lines from an inferior play and perhaps performing them badly at that. The tendency to formulate experience abstractly is a pattern that is an extension of the artist's persona, similar to the creation of a work of art. Yet outside the framework of creativity, it is a form of communication that impedes feeling and resists human contact.

Shakespeare's dilemma is how the artist, or any man of conscience assimilates moral knowledge in terms of experience. After Shakespeare witnesses the body of the gibbeted Young Woman, his face registers little expression, yet the vision of the girl's death crystalizes a series of images. Even her death polarizes responses from different segments of a stratified society. Viewed from each perspective, Bond anatomizes a culture that resists any sense of community or responsibility. Two farm laborers conjecture, "She died summa slow," and remain insulated from any sentiment by the spartan severity of their own lives. The Son's Puritan extremism is framed by an Old Testament religiosity that shrilly insists on its own righteousness and reduces experience to strict moral categories: "Lord god is wherever there's justice" (p. 22). Judith's perception of the girl's death is ridden with her own complicity; she intuitively recognizes that her action widens the gap between herself and her father: "Are you blaming me? Is that what I've done now?" (p. 24). The imagery of unrest and turbulence resolve in the Old Man's grotesque recollection of the riotous atmosphere that accompanies a public execution:

> O dear I hate a hanging. People runnin' through the streets laughin' an' sportin'. Buyin' and sellin'. I allus enjoyed the hanging when I was a boy. Now I can't abide 'em. The conjurors with red noses takin' animals out the air an' coloured things out their pockets. The soldier lads scare us. The parson an is antics. (p. 19)

Through each observor Bond reveals a stratified society that is recapitulated in the Old Man's speech. Yet the scene reveals a social process composed of multiple victimizations. Each witness resists personal involvement and detaches themselves from the spectacle of death, either intellectually, morally or emotionally.

Shakespeare literally turns his back on the others. Yet he is the only figure to acknowledge the implications of the scene and formulate a sympathetic response: "I thought I knew the questions. Have I forgotten them?" (p. 25). It is the first occasion of articulated self-doubt. He talks deliberately, as if to reassure himself against his own worst fears. The question yields to memory and an image of the world dragged down and tied to its own entrails. With the first intimation of recognition comes the guilt and self-reproach that had pressed upon the edges of his consciousness. Shakespeare's inexpressiveness functions as a type of emasculated potential, perhaps because he only mutely acknowledges what he has seen. Yet the consciousness of the artist has always been at work. What emerges is no longer neutrality or disengagement; that is impossible. The image that crystalizes reframes the world of the hanging and integrates the victimization of the baited bear with the Young Woman:

> The baited bear. Tied to the stake....Dried mud and spume. Men bringing dogs through the gate....Loose them and fight. The bear wonders around the stake....It knows it can't get away....Flesh and blood. Strips of skin. Teeth scraping bone....Round the stake. On and on...Howls...Roars...Men baiting their beast...And later the bear raises its great arm. The paw with a broken arm. And it looks as if it's making a gesture--it wasn't: only weariness and pain...Asking for one sign of grace....And the crowd roars for more blood and pain (p. 25).

The image of the bear is one of brutal persecution, yet Shakespeare utters the monologue objectively, mesmerized by the facticity of the events. The sheer horror inheres in the facts themselves, unmediated by the imagination. The artist himself seems a likely surrogate for the wounded bear: impotent, staked to a circumscribed lot of ground, unable to surmount the pain and weariness. But it is Judith's words, "You're only interested in your ideas" (p. 26), that impels Shakespeare to disclose what Bond has metaphorically prepared us for in the monologue of the bear-baiting, the Old Man's account of public execution and the gibbeting itself: "What does it cost to stay alive? I'm stupified at the suffering I've seen" (p. 26). The consciousness of the artist is the consciousness of any moral man in a universe of pain and suffering. From the inactivity and silence of the early scenes, Shakespeare has begun to think in terms of movement and action, and so succumbs to recognition and culpability: "There's no higher wisdom of silence" (p. 26). The words are quoted from the notebooks of Leonardo da Vinci, though the first draft reads, "There's no wisdom beyond your own responsiblity." Bond hypothetically reconstructs Shakespeare's response:

> I haven't really done anything, I haven't answered any of these problems and I haven't answered all those things that I want to, I haven't been able to set down solutions that make sense to anybody.[18]

The paradox, of course, is that the artist (Bond's version of him) who conceived *King Lear*, is wrenched out of his fictive self-containment and is filled with bewilderment: "I quiet the storms inside me. But the storm breaks outside" (p. 27). It is the revelation of the play that Shakespeare acknowledges the power of the artist to determine culture and bear the responsibility for his acts, yet can admit that he "usurped the place of God and lied" (p. 27). The dichotomy between the interior life of the artist and the responsible citizen who intercedes for the spiritual health of the community is formulated by Shakespeare's conflicts: the division between contemplation and action, art and activity, imagination and reality. By the middle of the play, he renounces his neutrality. Yet the split self is not so easily mediated. Bond purposely refashions a folk hero who is beset by the doubts and uncertainties of all other men; he is kind to his servents, generous without endangering his own interests, and would have preferred to aid the beggar woman. Shakespeare has always acknowledged the urgency of the issues but has repressed them for the sake of self-interest. Yet his position as a landowning member of the gentry permits him the opportunity to reflect. The Old Woman servant can only lament, "I yont afford to arkst question."

But the public figure also counters the instincts of the artist, who in epiphanic utterances half-consciously transforms reality onto a different plane of experience. In a moment of surface calm he narrates his encounter with a swan:

> A swan flew by me on the river. On a straight line just over the water....A woman running along an empty street. Its neck was rocking like a wave. I heard its breath when it flew by. The white swan and the dark water. Straight down the river and round a curve out of sight. I could still see its wing. God knows where it was going. (He goes to the gibbet.) Still perfect. Still beautiful. (pp. 27-28)

For a moment art merges with life. The experience of the hanging is transformed and aestheticized. The image of the swan becomes a metaphor for the life of abstract art--pure and clean as the words on a printed page. Direct and unimpeded, it is expressed without distraction by the imagination. Shakespeare's swan glides noiselessly, unencumbered by the presence of life below, the curve of its flight an image of a spirit barely pausing to glance at the reality it withdraws from. The gibbeted woman, marred by a brutal death remains aesthetically intact. Shakespeare's imagination functions as a safety valve, a means to somehow mediate reality and imaginatively transform the ugliness into the substance of recognition. Yet Shakespeare's words are counterpointed, and his voice at least partially called into doubt by the choric utterance of the Old Woman, who possesses a hard-headedness and an ability to penetrate the essential artificiality of his words: "Her's ugly. Her face al atwist...She smell" (p. 28).

The life of art, rather than the artistic process, is the subject of the confrontation between Shakespeare and Ben Jonson in Part Two of the play.

Shakespeare's acknowledgement that he writes nothing because he has nothing to say partially indicates the dislocation between art and experience. Jonson's life, on the other hand, has been a continual series of engagements in life. He unwittingly isolates the source of Shakespeare's discomfort when he complains, "What's your life like? Any real blood?....Life doesn't seem to touch you, I mean soil you....You are serene" (pp. 31-32). Unsurprisingly, the life of art seems to consume his powers without replenishing them. He shares Shakespeare's sense of powerlessness and verbalizes his colleague's silent thoughts and hidden regrets: "I go on and on. Why can't I stop? I even talk shit now. To know the seasons of life and death and quietly walk on the path between them" (p. 34). If he does not grasp the problem, he instinctively grasps its symptoms: "Something's happening to your will. You're being sapped" (p. 32). Shakespeare has uttered his thoughts in the context of the plays, yet he must articulate those beliefs in terms of action in order to validate the artist as a figure capable of sustaining culture.

Jonson's utterances provide an analogous frame of reference to the life of art in the play; writing is a process for each playwright that is hardly serene. Jonson as well as Shakespeare desires solitude and quiet as a measure of solace: "I hate writing. Fat white fingers excreting dirty black ink smudges, shadows, shit, silence..." (p. 31). Jonson's conception of the artistic process, all anguish and despair, reframes Shakespeare's vision of reality. Throughout the play, Shakespeare reflects on life like a merchant burdened by the realities of middle class existence: "The garden is too big," "Time goes on," "I'm surprised how old I've got." The tone is bourgeois, and familiar to any middle-class household breaking apart under duress and tension. By emphasizing Shakespeare's relatedness to all men, Bond constructs a framework of potential action for any citizen interested in the welfare of his community. Though Shakespeare and Jonson each despair, Jonson's felt existence has included four imprisonments, religious conversions, and finally murder. Part of Shakespeare's anguish is due to his disengagement with life. Yet both share the desperation of figures who remain sensitive to the truth, but stand passively aside.

Jonson's idyll, a reverie Shakespeare implicity shares, functions as an escape to myth: "To escape my life wandering through quiet fields. Charm fish from the water....Gather simple eggs. Muse with my reflection....And at last in some cool mossy grave" (p. 36). Bond creates an additional center of action to counterpoint the two writers , who at least possess the leisure to muse over the problematic nature of their perceptions, while a central action of the play--the dispossession of the farm laborers--occurs. Combe confronts the rebellious peasants who refuse to be displaced by "rich theives plunderin' the earth" (p. 35). The Son, the leader of the opposition, asks Combe, "Whose interst that protectin? Public or Yourn?" (p. 36). As the two antithetical class interests in the play confront one another, the two writers resign themselves to positions that have no bearing on the life of the community. As Combe expounds his views of cultural evolution to the Son, Shakespeare portentously slumps over, filled with drink:

> ...there'll always be real suffering, real stupidity and greed and violence. And there can be no civilization till you learn to live with it. I live in the real world and try to make it work. There's nothing more moral than that. But you live in a world of dreams. Well what happens when you wake up? You find that real people can't live in your dreams. They don't fit...they're not good or sane or noble enough (p. 36).

The monologue stands as a critique of Shakespeare's art and supports the ideology that capitalism is founded on a natural antagonism that is based on the exploitation of the weak by the strong. It's implied criticism is directed toward any idealist who believes that men can alter the shape of events. Shakespeare's humanism (in his art) undermines the "false culture" that prolongs itself by a distorted concept of human nature. Yet the realization that his implicit approval of the system endorses a corrupt bureaucracy becomes more and more impossible to endure. Shakespeare's exhaustion intimates not so much a narrowing of his powers but his diminution as a significant force in the life of the community. The two authors, one swaying drunkenly, the other unconscious imply the moderation of failed possiblity.

Part Five begins with the stage directions: "Open space. Flat white crispy empty. The fields, paths, roads, bushes and trees are covered with smooth, clean snow" (p. 29). Like an open, unwritten page, Bond conflates Shakespeare's impulse to act and the artistic process. Shakespeare idly muses over the empty landscape,

> How clean and empty the snow is. A sea without life. An empty glass. Still smooth. No footprints, no ruts. No marks of weapons or hoes dragged through the ground. Only my footprints behind me...white, white (p. 39).

In effect, he creates an image of his legacy to the world: a terrain untouched and unchanged by his powers. Bond remarks in an earlier draft: "Snow-perfect ideal. When it doesn't melt, WS lives in the perfect ideal. The perfect ideal is false because it is unreal. An ideal is always a lie."[19]

As Shakespeare recounts his mistakes, there is no reason for pretense or consolation, only the truth consoles. When the Son accidentally shoots his father, "Shakespeare," says Bond,

> ignores the wounded figure; this is the essence of his situation. Here he is drawn into the discovery of self-knowledge, so concentrated in his self-judgement, that you could probably set fire to his coat and he wouldn't notice it.[20]

For the first time, he is capable of addressing Judith with a measure of candor as he reveals a portion of his subjective, inner life:

> When I ran away from your mother and went to London--I was so bored. She's such a silly woman and you take after her. Forgive me. I know that's cruel and sordid but it's such an effort to be polite anymore....I love you with money....But money always turns to hate....I treated you so badly. I made you vulgar and cheap. I corrupted you. (p. 41)

Though he finally acknowledges complicity in the corruption of his daughter (the same way that Combe seduced him) even his contempt is aestheticized and detached:

> Don't be angry because I hate you, Judith. My hatred isn't angry. It's cold and formal. I wouldn't harm you. There's no limit to my hatred. It's destroyed too much to be satisfied so easily. Only truth can satisfy it now (p. 42).

Judith provokes her father's contempt and perhaps unfairly represents the irrationality of the world precisely because these issues possess no relevance for her. But attempting to be sane in an irrational society hardly absolves Shakespeare from having lived in conflict with his sense of values. His hatred is more likely self-directed and instigated by the separation between his instinctive humanism and a society that refuses to recognize his needs. Bond chose to write *Bingo* because of precisely these paradoxes. The figure who

> ...created Lear, who understands so much about suffering and violence, the partiality of authority, and the final innocence of all defenseless things and yet lives in a time when you could do nothing about it, then you feel the suffering you describe....When you write on that level you must tell the truth....So if you lie the world stops being sane, there is no difference between guilt and innocence and only the mad know how to live with so much despair.[21]

For Shakespeare, the tension between a seeking, creative interior life and the objective world of action results in the artist's willed demise. *Bingo* is the demonstration of certain truths about society which are rational and coherent. Society must bear the responsibility of its members; life as well as art aspires to moral sanity. Bond exhorts his audience to bring their daily lives in line with their aspirations, "the economic and political basis of society in line without ethical propaganda--we will then live in a condition of knowledge."²²

Shakespeare's silence resolves in a double suicide: artistic and human; each implies and complements the other. While silence signifies the absence of any created utterance (art), it also indicates Shakespeare's inability to engage or take an active role in the creation of community. The result, Bond implies, is the dispossession of the artistic as well as social self. Silence destroys the ethical structure which safeguards the human condition. Not even Shakespeare can create in an environment divested of human content.

While creativity satisfies an inner need for expression and is necessary to sustain culture, it cannot thrive sealed off from practical activity. Ultimately, Shakespeare fails; he is incapable of reclaimng the human in an alien world. He reacts ineffectively against a society ruled by laws of material production and is beseiged and cut off by an antagonistic society. The life of art abstracted from human activity is reduced to phrases: "White worms excreting black ink. Scratch. Scratch." Our final image is a limp figure twitching helplessly on the floor. Judith pronounces his legacy as she ransacks the room: "Nothing. Nothing. Nothing." Yet in a final utterance, Shakespeare is capable of declaring, "Every writer writes in other men's blood. There's nothing else to write in. But only a god or a devil can write in other men's blood and not ask why they spilt it and at what cost" (p. 43). Not surprisingly, it is Combe who presides over Shakespeare's demise when he casually hands him tablets from Jonson's poison bottle. The polarity is clear, if overstated: Combe emerges as the villain and the most significant agent of social energy in the play. In one gesture, Bond crystalizes Shakespeare's last confrontation and capitulation to the ruling class. Yet the taking of his own life is a refusal, finally, to be a part of such a system, rather than the disillusioned gesture of a sterile aesthete. His final refrain, "Was anything done?" acknowledges his altered vision as well as a measure of self-blame. Unlike the Son, Shakespeare refuses, though belatedly, to deceive himself; he remains self-critical, finally assured that "morality can exist only in a culture or be forged in the quest for one."[23]

ENDNOTES

[1] Hay and Roberts, p. 198.

[2] Hay and Roberts, eds., *Edward Bond: A Companion to the Plays* (London: T.Q. Publications, 1978), p. 59.

[3] K.H. Stoll, "Interview with Edward Bond and Arnold Wesker," *Twentieth Century Literature*, 22 (1976), p. 420.

[4] Edward Bond, *Bingo and the Sea* (New York: Hill and Wang, 1975), p. 31.

[5] Op. cit., No. 3, p. 421.

[6] Ibid, p. 422.

[7] Hay and Roberts, p. 199.

[8] Op. cit., No. 2, p. 21. p. 21.

[9] Op. cit., No. 3, p. 420

[10] "Introduction," *Bingo*, p. xiii.

[11] Ibid, pp. xii-xiii.

[12] Op. cit., No. 2, p. 46.

[13] Ibid, p. 62.

[14] Ibid, p. xvi.

[15] Op. cit., No. 10, p. xvi.

[16] Op. cit., No. 3, p. 418.

[17] Op. cit., No. 10, p. xvi.

[18] Op. cit., No. 2, p. 59.

[19] Op. cit., No. 7, p. 195.

[20] Ibid, p. 195.

[21] Op. cit, No. 10, p. x.

[22] Op. cit., No. 2, p. 52.

[23] Edward Bond, "Introduction," *The Fool* (Chicago: The Dramatic Publishing Co., 1976), p. vii.

Chapter 4

THE FOOL: THE ARTIST AND COMMERCIAL CULTURE

The publication of John Clare's first volume of poetry, *Poems Descriptive of Rural Life and Scenery*, resulted in a great deal of notoriety when it was issued in 1820. However, literary celebrity was short-lived and perhaps a matter of curiosity on the part of the 19th-century literary and social establishment. No longer stylish and quickly foresaken, Clare was forced to work as a farm laborer to support his family. The last years of his life were spent in lunatic asylums in Epping and Northampton.

In the widest sense, Bond uses the story of Clare's life to examine the idea of a pastoral golden age that mythifies the quaintness of peasant life in rural England. More specifically, Clare's life suggests how political judgments lay concealed behind aesthetic ones and how the artist is entrapped by a system of aristocratic patronage and the machinery of a capitalist, commercial culture.

For Clare, creative and artistic freedom is a measure of the poet's relation to his social and political environment. Through art, man grasps his own reflection in a world he has imaginatively constructed. But in the social structure of *The Fool*, art loses its capacity to express the artist's creative energy; Clare's dilemma lies beyond the sphere of creativity and in the socioeconomic relations he has with the world.

In the play, Bond examines how the laws of material production are extended to artistic creation. Bourgeois culture demands an art that endorses a concept of the world that corresponds to its own class interests. When

Clare refuses to be coerced into a relationship with society which is independent of his will, when he insists on creating in response to an inner need for expression rather than making concessions that would delimit his artistic activity, he finds himself in contradiction with an economic system into which his art has been absorbed. Yet the artist cannot cease to create, even when his art is reduced to the condition of a speculative asset and is stripped of its human significance. Clare creates out of necessity--to satisfy a human need for self-expression; he can't be silent without undermining the rationale which guarantees his moral sanity.

Unfortunately, his attempt to humanize his surroundings results in his own dehumanization and "spiritual" dispossession: an inability to experience himself as the acting agent in his relationship with the world. Clare emerges as a significant and personalized voice whose refusal to endorse the dominant ideology is reflected in his search for an artistic form to express his resistance. Though he cannot precisely grasp the historical significance of the events--"human consciousness is class consciousness"--Clare's relations with society embody the contradiction between material existence and creative necessity when the work of art and its distribution is controlled by powers other than the artist. Clare's refusal to be dominated by that power structure suggests the dilemma of any artist engaged in his activity at the sufferance of political institutions that regulate art. The more Clare critically appropriates the external world in his art, the more unsparing he becomes and the less society is willing to endure his claims. In the play, the artist's relation to his art shifts from ownership to dispossession, much like the relationship of the agricultural class to the land. The transforming power of art itself is no longer suffficient to sustain the artist's survival. When his creativity is experienced as no longer belonging to him, estrangement takes its ultimate form--madness.

Clare's art is market-oriented when it submits to the exigencies of the market--the fluctuations of supply and demand. When he refuses to heed those demands, when art becomes a level of merchandise and falls under the laws of production, the process of creative activity is subverted, especially when such activity is the artist's only means of subsistence. The opposition between capitalism and creativity is a product of a social environment where relationships have become impersonal and reified; the artist himself becomes an object and interest in his art lies in its utility rather than in its objectification of human content.

Clare, for instance, is not individuated until fairly late in the play. At that point, Bond diverts our attention from a class society undergoing drastic revision to the particular destruction of a single figure who refuses to conform to the capitalist relations society demands. In the first half of the play, Bond elaborates the dynamic and quality of life which Clare is born into, matures in, and is finally animated by. In the second half, he reflects on its emblem--the visionary artist who merges the private and the political, the individual and the historical. For Bond, the fool of the play's title incarnates the paradox of Clare's life. Martin Esslin suggests that the play's title signifies a "passive central character...who sees the world revolve around him without fully understanding what's happening."[1] Clare is certainly a fool to society for trying to recreate reality in a shape that the ruling class fails to ratify; his refusal to compromise and his ability to arrive at a critical evaluation of himself and his environment imply that he is a fool to a culture whose values he rejects. At the same time, he is self-deceived by his personal illusions and is incapable of providing the impetus for the evolution of a working-class culture that implements the creation of a rational society. In his early notes, Bond argues that the fool suggests "kinship with characters like the Fool in *Lear* and Ariel in *The Tempest*"[2] and reflects a sense of "knowing resilience." Though Clare comes to possess the consciousness to reorder his thinking, it comes too late to provide the impetus for change. More explicitly, the parallel with Shakespeare's fools suggests the way artists are "emasculated by their dependent relations with their patrons. In fact, they are granted immunity from censure by virture of their role."[3] The implication is that the way "society views the function of art invariably determines its effect."[4]

Clare's art comes to represent a portion of society that is collectively unable to oppose a rigid, hierarchical power structure. In response, society almost reflexively opposes the artist as he resists reification. For Bond, human misery, rather than an a natural fault, lies in its rootedness in a class system; this "class nature distorts human consciousness and is responsible for the myths that pervert culture."[5] Clare refuses to integrate his art in the quantified and banal universe of bourgeois society and opposes society through his faithfullness to his creative will. Creation implicitly comes to mean rebellion. As his existence is progressively denied, he feels the need to express his humanity outside the dominant social and political institutions. Yet economically, he must create within the range of possibilities offered by a particular social structure. Clare experiences actual physical pangs when he refuses to compromise by laboring in the fields in order to maintain a slender livelihood. Yet it is a single and impossible gesture of resistance. By inscribing himself on the endless scraps of paper Patty labels "scribble," he has at least guaranteed a human presence in a world ruled by quantitative criteria. However, he can only reconcile his own conflicts by recognizing and attempting to resolve the dilemmas posed by society. What

Clare learns is that the dehumanization of men has its correlative in the dehumanization of art. In a sense, he takes on a task for which his powers are inadequate. Clare has created in opposition to the power structure and has barricaded himself in his creative will. Yet for Bond, the artist has no choice: an understanding of the nature of society is a prerequisite to any judgment he might make about himself--the anguish of noncompliance is in part the legacy of the creative imagination. Unlike Shakespeare, Clare represents no field of conflicted doubts and uncertainties. His madness is metaphorically a function of what society has done to him, rather than a self-induced paralysis over his failure to act. He is not finally destroyed by any internal complication but through his failure to relinquish his vision. He is isolated by his own community and by social forces in which human connections dissolve without the economic substance to sustain them. For Clare, and all the other characters in the play, there is no sense of community capable of sustaining itself. Bond demonstrates how society becomes divided by fundamental contradictions and hence how relationships within that framework erode when they assume the form of relationships among "things." Darkie's inability to communicate with the Parson, Milton's denunciation of his son, Clare's misreading of his relationship with Mary, and even Patty's ingenuous reproof of Clare's art indicate the reciprocity of destructiveness implicit in relationships under capitalism. Ironically, it is the artist who is put away and isolated from the social continuum because he is too in touch with human specificity. Clare's imprisonment is the inevitable response of a social structure unable and unwilling to assimilate knowledge of its own self-destructiveness.

In the first half of the play, John Clare is set haphazardly against a background that functions to question the price of survival in an age corroded by economic and political corruption; what the ruling class and subsequent historians have termed an "age of transition." More an undifferentiated member of an agricultural laboring class that is exploited by sectional and class interests, Clare functions neither as a figure with artistic aspirations nor as the spokesman for an embattled working class culture. In fact, he seems rather indifferent to the social protest that surrounds him. He neither disclaims the imminent changes that the enclosures will produce or contemplates the injustice of the events. Instead, Bond portrays him as a philanderer--romantic and full of sexual energy.

The Mummer's playlet that begins *The Fool* is a prologue to the main action and sets the tone for the idea of loss and passage. It is the incursion of a former age in which a culturally unified laboring class sought and derived solace from the protection and paternalistic attitude the gentry adopted. The idea of the play itself, as well as its East Anglican dialect, suggests a cultural integrity that is starkly contrasted to the rhetorical formality of the gentry's mechanical responses. Bond uses the language of the community because

> of its curious concrete feel, it's repetitive, it's like a hammer, knocking, knocking...but at the same time, it can be very agile and witty. It's a language which imitates experience. Because language shouldn't be just words, it should be something that moves in the mouth and forces gestures and action.[6]

The play-within-a-play creates an ironic and prophetic counterpoint to the fate of Clare, particularly if the actor portraying Clare impersonates the Doctor. In an oblique parody of his own victimization, the Doctor exploits a wounded knight--"Ten pounds if he's rich, twenty pounds if he's poor"[7] --and recites doggerel which foreshadows the dissolution of Clare's own creative instincts at the end of the play. Like the Doctor he portrays, Clare is unable to bring comfort to members of his own class.

Power has accumulated in the hands of Lord Milton, the land owner to whom the working class has entrusted its secular interests, and the Parson, the spokesman for the ontological well-being of the community. Each provides formal and elaborately worded apologias for the dismemberment of the rights and principles of working-class culture. The change in tone after the Mummer's play is particularized by the Parson's weighty pronouncements after polite, ritualized applause from the gathered nobility. It is an abrupt punctuation to the play, and formally marks off the transition from a pastoral age to an industrial one:

> England is beset by troubles....We are entering a new age. An iron age. New engines, new factories, cities, wage laws. The old ways must go. Our land must be bettter used....All of us must be patient and understanding. We must work for the common good." (p. 6)

The sense of stasis and tradition in the Mummer's play is paired off against the sense of motion and progressiveness of the Parson's words. Bond remarks that,

> He's probably consciously preparing the Parish for the changes Milton's going to make. The Parson has probably been buttering them up for some time now--they almost expect hints. But they don't really understand it, it hasn't been spelt out insofar as it affects them."[8]

Like Combe in *Bingo*, the Parson's exhortations seem logical if abstracted from the circumstances; in actuality, they are the means which the ruling class ideologically seeks to maintain its ascendency. The emphasis on a vague, collective solidarity and goodwill rationalizes a series of measures designed to control the working class. Yet the unanimity of goodwill is undermined as we listen to Lord Milton's arguments. His reliance on the laws of economic science darkly conclude that "Civilization costs money like everything else" (p. 7), and creates uncertainty about a figure who seeks to establish himself, along with the Parson, as a center of proletariat trust. Linguistically, Bond plots three modes of expression that evolve from the native voice of the laboring class, to the ceremonious words of the Parson, to the bureaucratic absolutism of Lord Milton. The Church of England and capitalism will maintain their ascendency if the working class entrusts itself to the Lord's will and values the paternal wisdom of the ruling class. Each relies on a power structure that loftily concludes "Our rulers guide our affairs in such a way that each of us reaps the best possible reward for his labors" (p. 7).

For the first third of the play, Bond strategically places Clare's countryman, Darkie, at the center of moral protest and intentionally shifts the audience's focus away from the poet of the play's title. Darkie intuitively grasps the historical momentousness of the events and aggressively protests the displacement of the farm laborers. Clare wanders indifferently in and out of the first few scenes preoccupied, more a purveyor of feeling than thought. He remains unconverted, perhaps still in his creative infancy and driven by no impulse other than self-gratification. His only gestures are amorous and even then his attentions are distributed among various amours. Yet, as we come to observe, the attention Bond devotes to Clare's non-artistic preoccupations is the agency through which he fuses the personal with the historical.

Bond introduces us to Clare, the artist, unceremoniously, almost as an afterthought. The stage directions read: "Clare alone. He sits. His lips move and his fingers tap a rhythm. He is saying something noiselessly to himself" (p. 10). It is a wonderfully slight and unannounced gesture. And when Clare begins to speak, his words have little to do with poetry. Instead, they focus on the permutations of his romantic intrigues. Nothing more is revealed than a figure beset by a romantic impulse towards a bawdy serving girl he had encountered in the first scene: "Never seen a girl like you. Like t'live in the forests. The two of us. Tread the reeds..." (p. 15). Yet Mary only prosaically responds to Clare's sexual energy and not at all to his imagination.

It is the first indication, and one that Bond hardly draws attention to so early in the play, that a portion of Clare's selfhood is based on delusions about himself. His insistence on a life of illusion and self-absorption, whether to seduce a working girl or to explicate the conflict between the rural working class and the gentry, neutralizes his voice. Ironically, it is his infatuation and pursuit of Mary which prevents his imprisonment during one of the play's most critical confrontations.

Led by Darkie, a group of laborers release their frustration by confronting the Parson in a dark wood. Yet, Bond comments, the gesture fails because, "It's no more than a spontaneous resistance to legalized robbery."[9] The episode is concretized in the image of Darkie's threat of retaliation: "Fraid I put my fist in your face? Hev a fist in my face all day" (p. 25). Darkie is the movement's most dynamic spokesman and possesses the energy and will to act, but he is powerless if the rural community does not act collectively. When he is confronted and arrested by Milton, he anatomizes the prerogative of the gentry in their interaction with the working class: "You steal from us. Parson steal from us. When I steal from Parson what you do t'me. Law hang us. Thass the on'y difference t'when you an' me: you on't think twice 'fore you use violence" (p. 28). The struggle for survival in a narrowing space is the preeminent objective of nearly everyone in the play. Bond infuses this idea with a special particularity by incorporating a series of material and physical impressions: images of abundance and starvation alternate with a narrowing sense of physical space that is diminished by the circumscription of the land and successive locations of enclosure and imprisonment: the prison, Clare's garden, and the claustrophobia of the madhouse.

The irrationality of society, its division according to class, and the violence and exploitation that provides the basis for its relationships are elaborated in the rest of the play through the life of Clare. It is not surprising that a prison is the location for the disclosure of Clare's recognition as an artist and the madhouse is the site of his final public utterance. Patty, who will denounce the idea of her husband's creativity by the middle of the play, proudly announces, "Scribblin come t'summat. Gen'man him talk bout a book" (p. 30). Yet the subject of Clare's words are not motivated by concern for the imprisonment of Darkie or the rebellious farmers. When Miles asks, "What you write boy...about this place. What goo on?" (p. 31). Clare dispassionately retorts, "Who'd read that" (p. 31). As if to punctuate and condemn his neutrality, the Parson enters and expounds upon the imperfectibility of man and the futility of optimism. Bond's strategy is designed to explore the way dominant institutions and certain myths are formulated to oppress and control human beings:

> If you don't die at the end of the week you will die in time....Forget this world, its misery and waste, all luxury and vice....Hope is a tool that goes in and out and grinds men together till they wear each other down. (p. 31)

Though Darkie is about to be executed and Patty, Clare's fiance, is standing by his side, Clare insists on inquiring about his former mistress. In his own mind she has become an emblem of obsessive preoccupation, an image of misdirection. Bond tells us that

> Clare wants to romanticize her--to see her as a body without a critical mind, merely an assenting mind. But she judges, makes decisions. She's too strong to fit into her situation, but not strong enough, perceptive, or organized enough (how could she be) to change it....Clare thinks she knows about freedom and happiness in a way he doesn't--in a way outside reality, above the constraints of living in or off society, but she doesn't really know either.[10]

The entire scene is set off by Clare's fits of hysterical laughter to which it seems difficult to assign precise meaning. Patty attributes Clare's behavior to selfishness, but Darkie faintly intuits its remoteness. Ultimately, the sound of laughter is echoed by other voices until it "spirals up inside the prison." The laughter itself is self-contained and there is no preparation or reference to it afterwards. Rather, it functions metaphorically as a container of one of the play's central images: the idea of the fool. Whether its object is the absurdity of the events, Clare's pointed indifference, or is even self-mockingly directed at himself, its mingling with other voices within the prison creates a texture of indifference to the fate of the men about to be judged. The laughter ringing in Clare's ears perhaps even mocks his own aspirations and subtly prophesizes his future.

Bond sets the fifth scene in Hyde Park, where Clare, recognized for his artistic promise, is introduced to polite society. The scene unfolds like the editing of a piece of film; our focus alternates from Clare and Mrs. Emmerson exchanging pleasantries downstage, to an upstage arena in which an Irishman and a black man hammer each other at the behest of their upper-class backers. The multiple focus enables the audience to analyze events in which two sets of victims are exploited by a self-serving system which seduces its victims through a series of well-concealed deceptions. The complicity of an old cockney and a Marquis who join to capitalize on the defeat of the Irishman serves as the background for the selling out of Clare. Bond explains that

> All these people in the front scene are Clare's patrons and upstage these boxers are knocking themselves to death to please their patrons, their backers. What I am saying, of course, is that the people in the front are really the same sort of people as in the back. Clare's patrons are in fact destroying him because they are not really interested in his art. It's an irony which I carry throughout the scene.[11]

Mrs. Emmerson, who courts the poet and basks in his celebrity, encourages a genteel art that her social position approves. Looking after the "child-like artist" is a civic duty that the inspired "song teller" deserves: "We have grass and trees in this park. Do they not inspire you?" (p. 39). Despite her attentiveness, "It is my ambition to be at your side when the muse calls.

I shall take down your words as you cast them in the air" (p. 39), Clare is not an innocent confounded by an urban landscape. Yet his prospects seem to be ominously poised against a series of subtle images and indirect confrontations in the scene. While we still cannot measure the growth of any moral imagination in the figure who shyly accepts Mrs. Emmerson's praise, the two boxers pummel one another urged on by threats from their corners. The scene is choreographed to include the destiny of another poet, whose fate augurs badly for Clare. Charles Lamb, destitute and alcoholic--"He can't suport his sister and marry so he drinks" (p. 40), confides Mrs. Emmerson--portentously utters his own judgement: "Clare tells the truth" (p. 42), he concludes, which "isn't governed by the laws of supply and demand..." (p. 43). Lamb continues enigmatically, yet his words are an implicit warning about a society which turns truth to profit: "Truth is often ugly. The spit on God's face...it's even more dangerous when the truth is told by a wise man" (p. 43). Admiral Radstock, author of *The British Flag Triumphant*, and a more influential patron, finds Clare's poetry effective in terms of its verisimilitude; yet his remarks are instinctively dominated by his stature, and his reknown as a "benefactor": "Your verse. Great charm there. True melody. Fine love of English landscape...a soldier or Christian may read it with profit" (p. 45). However, he insists on dictating artistic control and admits he has reservations about lines "which criticize the landowning class" and "smack of radicalism." Mrs. Emmerson repreminds the "naughty child" when she breezily recites verse that redeem the philanderer of the first four scenes: "Accursed wealth/ O'er bounding human laws/ Of every evil then remains the cause" (p. 46). For Radstock and Mrs. Emmerson, art is designed to satisfy the pseudo-aesthetic needs of an emasculated, reified consciousness. Capitalism prefers to make Clare's art serve the needs of mass-consumption. From an ideological point of view, it is the most effective way of preserving the alienating relations between capitalism and society. Capitalist expropriation (in terms of the enclosure) in *The Fool* and *Bingo* not only put an end to a way of life but also expropriate the artist's creative essence. The laws of the market reduce Clare's creative vitality to a local and picturesque phenomenon. Yet Clare's imagination has been politicized and generates a confrontation with the Admiral whose censure of Clare's subversive politics is a device he uses to protect his own interests. His plea for order is really for authority--"Who controls the brute in man? Polite society....your verse undermines its authority. There'd be chaos. The poor would be the first to suffer" (p. 48). More significantly for Clare's future, Radstock argues, "The people you criticize are the only ones who can afford books. The only ones who can read" (p. 48). Paradoxically, political freedom is the cost of continuing as the emergent spokesman for what Clare has digested and formalized through art: "O'nt see no nymphs in our fields, but I see a workhouse" (p. 48), he retorts to Radstock. Part of Clare's dilemma is that he seeks solace from a society that he remains critical of. Unlike Shakespeare, who seems to possess at least a dim awareness of historical process, Clare doesn't comprehend the absurdity of trying to maintain economic survival in a social environment that he seeks to indict.

The functionless subjectivity of art is crystalized by Mrs. Emmerson's response when she naively asks, "How does it help to shake your fist at heaven when some homeward wending swain perishes in the snow?" (p. 48). Lamb punctuates the moment by uttering cynically, "Spitting on God's mask." Yet even his words reflect the ambiguous status of the artist. The words are uttered obliquely, in metaphoric obscurity because, Mrs. Emmerson presumes, of his preeminence as an artist: "I'm proud to say I didn't understand a single word. Mr.

Lamb, you're a poet. You have no call to go round putting ideas in people's heads" (p. 49).

What particularizes Clare is the way Bond creates a figure full of promise yet torn by contradiction. Despite his capacity to reveal an unjust society, he remains personally committed to his illusions. One portion of his consciousness has confronted the external world with imagination, yet Clare remains unable to divest himself of his romantic illusion. It is an obstacle the artist must overcome if he is to mediate his vision of the world with the materials of his own reality.

When Bond redirects our attention to the conclusion of the boxing match with a description of the Irishman about to be knocked senseless, he choreographs in visual images the fate of Clare at the end of the play: "He sways slowly to his feet, like a half-drowned man forcing himself to make useless gestures....He's unable to give up" (p. 49). Lamb cries out, "the cost," and Mrs. Emmerson busies herself with obtaining tickets for a concert whose program will set Clare's lyrics to music. The image is prophetic of Clare's subsequent confinement to a madhouse. In fact, he is so drawn to the defeated Irishman that their exchange, brief, but heavy with irony, comes to reflect Clare's own destiny. He cannot resist inquiring, "O'not knew a man could stand so much....You keep comin back" (p. 52). Jackson replies, "Then ain't I the bigger fool?" It is a touching moment and a climax of sorts, a brief union between a lost cause and one soon to be lost, a communion and a commiseration of shared despair.

By the next scene, five years later, Clare's optimism has been transformed by the public's indifference. Patty, uncomprehending and unable to grasp the extent of her husband's privation, describes the fate of the artist who possesses no utility other than creativity, no scruple other than a refusal to compromise:

> Look at thass child John Clare. Thass sick an pukin...cause thass famished like its mother. An its father....For what. Scribble. Scribble. Scribble. Scribble on bits of paper for rats t'eat. Scribble. Scribble. Scribble. (p. 56)

Clare, like Shakespeare, cannot find any solace in his garden, but unlike Shakespeare, he cannot afford the luxury of remaining there. In *Bingo*, the division between knowledge and action is understood intellectually by Shakespeare, partly through his membership in the ruling class; he at least possesses the luxury of addressing the right issues. For Clare, knowledge and action are more intuitive and affective. His unself-consciousness is in part the result of his class origins. He remains an instinctive artist who is neither in a position to recognize or react to the historical process that creates the gap between material survival and politically undesirable art. What remains is the painful image of Clare forlornly peeling potatoes, divested of what he barely possessed as Patty scornfully intones, "God hang the man that invented ink" (p. 54)--a variation on Jonson's remarks about authorship--"white worms excreting black ink." The exigencies of survival even deny Patty the right to contemplate the idea of poetry. Pulled apart by an ideolgoical base whose demands are at odds with his principles, Clare laments:

> Can't help what I am. God knows I wish I couldn't write my name....O' God 'ont even know if thass truth any more. No grip left in my hand. 'Ont go back laborin...'ont know what I'm about in the fields. Pain in my head. (p 55)

It is the fate of the artist who has no means to express his vision--the imagination is an autonomous activity that the artist is incapable of controlling. Creative necessity remains an irresistable impulse; even Clare's words become oppressive as they seek expression: "Hundreds o verse....Chorus in my head all day. Each sings a different tune" (p. 58). The absurdity of his publisher's demand of payment for discounted sales from Clare himself, and the suggestion of the "faithful" Mrs. Emmerson to sell extra copies to the illiterate villagers, further refutes the rationality of the social order. Clare's poems stand beyond his grasp when they exist independent and outside his control. They stand opposed to him as autonomous powers in what Marx labels separation through surrender: the loss of one's product and labor to the forces of the marketplace. With a measure of self-recognition, Clare addresses an impersonal universe: "Hev the world gone mad? No wonder they say I'm a clown" (p. 59). While Mrs. Emmerson elaborates on the expense of decoding his "scribble" for polite society, Clare lurches into a hallucinatory trance that somehow retains a visionary lucidity. He still maintains faith in the efficacy of Mary, "the other one...all I want is t'lay my head on her breast. Peace then. Laugh again. Talk like a sensible man. I'm so alone" (p. 63). In addition to the social structures that constrict Clare's life, his preoccupation with Mary--a symbol of naive idealism--must be stripped away. He must achieve a measure of cognition before he can redress his own conception of the world.

When Lord Milton requests that Clare recite one of his verses, however, the poet approaches the limit of his self-knowledge in one field of action:

> You 'ont know how to listen. 'Ont write for you. 'Ont be a poet then....Shall I step in line now? No, 'ont labor in your fields....I've eat my portion of the universe an I shall die of it....But had more out the stones in your field than you had out the harvest." (pp. 63-64)

Unlike Shakespeare, Clare remains an unredeemed idealist, even though he does nothing to transform society outside the utterances of his art. Neither is he a passive fatalist; he remains inflexible in the confrontation of wills with Milton and the power structure he represents. Though Milton does not consciously intend to hurt Clare, social pressures once set in motion, compel his actions. With a measure of some relief he pays the expense to have Clare's incoherence officially sanctioned.

Not surprisingly, a representative of the power structure attends to Clare's rehabilitation; Dr. Skrimshire attempts to "disentangle the truth from the poetry" (p. 64). But society remains incapable of assimilating self-knowledge. The idea of poetry and its association with truth--"What I wrote was good. Yes. Worth readin" (pp. 63-64)--reminds the reader of Lamb's misgivings, just as the figure of a doctor who seeks to anatomize the integrity of a work of art is reminiscent of the quack figure portrayed by Clare in the Mummer's play. The boxing image, which years earlier had insinuated itself in Clare's consciousness, is a useful metaphor for a society dominated by incessant combat--"They git paid for being knocked about, I git knocked about....Why I 'ont paid for it?" (p. 60), Clare queries as Milton locks his arms and actualizes the metaphor. His final plea, "You can't drag me out of my garden" (p. 65), is an ironic gloss on Shakespeare's refusal to leave the safety and solitude of his garden.

In a grotesque parody of the efficacy of art, Patty timidly inquires, "Was he a proper writer?" Mrs. Emmerson responds melodramatically, but her words possess a measure of logic: "At first--but perhaps they became only ramblings, droolings....O this terrible day. He was so brave. He did so much but he couldn't even get a living like any rough" (p. 66). In the end, the need for art is undermined by material circumstances. Clare's moral imagination is resisted by the gentry as well as by a stolid member of his own class. Art is nullified by a set of conditions which neither permit the artist freedom to live nor to create. Patty's conclusion possesses an air of finality and hard-headed practicality towards creative activity. She comments ingenuously to Mrs. Emmerson: "His books learn you how t'starve. 'Ont need books t'learn that" (p. 66).

Only after the self-recognition of a hallucinatory experience that is half dream and half projection of his own uncertainties can Clare rid himself of self-deception and compose the poems addressed to Mary in the afterward of the text: "You are a poet and should have known/ You must imagine the real and not the illusion....Clare, you created illusions and they destroy poets" (pp. 86-87).

In the central scene of the play, Clare escapes briefly from the asylum. Alone and exhausted, he confronts the shadows of his own imagination, the guilt and illusion he must overcome before he is finally freed of them. Bond clarifies the dynamics of the scene:

> He argues his way through the scene, he seeks out reasons and understanding, he doesn't just say it's all fantasy, illusion, a madhouse: he explains why things went wrong and what will happen next. Clare is a rational man, in this mad scene, even more than at other times....it's terrifying that the people who have power are so irrational...but in the meantime he will have written the poems, that is: he will have made the world more rational, he will have written rational lines on the face of madmen....Clare's is a voice of sanity in a mad world.[12]

The Mary he imaginatively encounters is no longer sexually desirable but "grotesque, filthy and ugly," a woman he trades for bread and a bit of cheese. While Clare seeks to mediate truth and dream, Mary admits that Clare is simply the boy who got her sacked. Her declaration allows Clare to make his own: "I give it all away for you. Patty, kids, my whole life. All away....That drove me mad" (p. 68). Just as Mary refuses his idealized love, the apparition of Darkie, a brutalized image of a boxer, is neither loyal nor a friend. Both Mary and Darkie persist as indictments of what is done to man through the way the artist imaginatively conceives them. Each functions as a projection of what Clare has become. The artist gropes toward self-awareness by projecting images in the guise of a haggard female figure and a blind boxer who is incapable of eating--the most basic human activity. Clare finally realizes, "No.

No one is there. Never way. 'Ony the songs I make up on them" (p. 74).

In a process of self-recognition and clarification, the artist comes to terms with his own guilt, and also with a potential solution:

> I wandred round an' round....We should have come t'gither. She git the bread. He crack the heads when they come after us. An' I--I'd hev teach him how to eat. I am a poet an' I teach men how to eat. Then she 'ont go in rags. He 'ont go blind. An' I 'ont go mad in a madhouse." (pp. 73-74)

"Bread and love" alone are insufficient, but the voice of the poet intuits a wholeness out of partialness, a complete social vision that integrates Darkie's spirit of resistance, Mary's inspiration and his own measure of wisdom. It is the poet's function to see collectively; he remains the eyes of the community. As the play concludes, however, Clare's voice is barely audible. He is reduced to a shrivelled puppet whose head nods like a broken doll. But the madhouse is also the site of Milton's self-revelation when he accompanies Patty on a visit to her husband. The oppressor is oppressed in the network of values that comprise the capitalist power structure--"I can't sleep....The dawn hurts my eyes. I hate my son, a vicious bastard. I was cruel sometimes. Foolish. But did I hate?" (pp. 76-77). The moment is brief, the vision incomplete, and the self-knowledge only partial. Unfettered, Clare might have been able to provide a response to Milton's query. But Milton has torn down the safeguards for his own sanity. He is, as Bond comments, "also a derelict...he is a gentleman and at the same time a sort of cultural psychopath who has destroyed almost everyone he's touched."[13]

It is finally Patty who pronounces Clare's epitaph: "Sorry you on't had a proper life. Us hev t'make the most of what there is" (p. 79). Patty's candid admission is poised against the Doctor's complaint that Clare shared some complicity in Milton's premature departure. "Clare," he demands, "have you made trouble?" (p. 80). It is a final irony for the beleagured artist, isolated and stricken by a class that makes art (and culture) impossible in relation to society.

ENDNOTES

[1] Martin Esslin, "Nor Yet a Fool to Fame," *Theatre Quarterly*, 6, No. 21 (1970), p. 44.

[2] Hay and Roberts, p. 203.

[3] Jenny S. Spencer, "Edward Bond's Dramatic Strategies," in *Contemporary English Drama*, ed. C.W.E. Bigsby (New York: Holmes and Meier Pub., 1981), p. 135.

[4] Ibid, p. 136.

[5] *Companion*, p. 74.

[6] Tony Coult, "Edward Bond: Creating What Is Normal," *Plays and Players*, 23, No. 3 (December 1975), p. 11.

[7] Edward Bond, *The Fool* p. 4

[8] Op. cit., No. 5, p. 74.

[9] Op. cit., No. 2, p. 203.

[10] Op. cit., No. 5, p. 65.

[11] Beverly Matherne and Salvatore Maiorana, "An Interview with Edward Bond," *Kansas Quarterly*, 12, No. 4. 69.

[12] Op. cit., No. 5, p. 66.

[13] Ibid, p. 66.

Chapter 5

THE BUNDLE: THE ARTIST AS ANY MAN

When I wrote my first plays, I was naturally conscious of the strength of human beings to provide answers. The answers are not always light and easy or even straight-forward, but the purpose--a socialist theatre--is clear.¹

Performed in 1978, ten years after the production of *Narrow Road to the Deep North: A Comedy*, *The Bundle* represents a transformation of artistic purpose--a commitment from pacifism and non-violent change to a commitment to revolutionary socialism. In the "Preface," Bond elaborates a dramatic method that had taken ten years to evolve and had spanned the politicization of the English intellectual community by events in Vietnam, Ireland, and a drastically failing economy. The dramatic method of *The Bundle* presents the audience with a "dramatisation of the analysis instead of the story."² If art has become a function of the need to interpret experience rather than to submit to it, Bond's reformulation suggests a preoccupation with the political response of an audience and a socialist point of view:

> ...merely recounting an event or telling a story on stage will not provide the opportunity for a correct interpretation of the event or story or the people involved. These may be misinterpreted...because many of the audience will not be politically conscious and so will not understand the event or story or even the moral content. (p. xiv)

Bond's dialectical analysis suggests an increased attentiveness to the political consciousness of the audience and implies, like Brecht before him, that the playwright who merely tells a story cannot confront the audience with the urgency of the tranforming process (the conditions under which people are governed, their material well-being and the terms under which they survive as a species). In a world where "interpretation is counterfeited by society" (p. xv), Bond's dramatic purpose is to draw attention to the inequities between a humanistic, rational society and the institutionalized capitalism that creates an alienated social order.

The Bundle, therefore, is best understood not as a "story of Wang but as a demonstration of how the words 'good' and 'bad' and moral concepts in general work in society and how they ought to work if men are to live rationally..." (p. xviii). The audience experiences these moments of crisis not as passive witnesses but as a collective figure more informed than the actors on stage. They possess the transforming energy of "interpretors of experience, agents of the future, restoring meaning to action" (p. xx). As the first of Bond's answer plays, *The Bundle* generates the optimism that theatre can reformulate, if not create self-consciousness and oppose society's institutionalization.

If *Narrow Road to the Deep North* sought to make queries about the function of the artist in order to dialectically demonstrate the rational laws of society, *The Bundle* provides a darker response to the symbiotic relation of the artist to his environment. No longer subtitled *A Comedy*, *New Narrow Road to the Deep North* (the new subtitle) provides a scenario in which Basho incorporates fewer roles and functions. In his latest incarnation, Basho has been transformed from a figure of blunted and frustrated pedagogy. He no longer resembles a picaresque and accidental sojourner distorted into an irresponsible Don Quixote.

In the first play, Bond's inability to clarify his own artistic purpose resulted in the creation of a figure who functioned successively as an ironist, a choric figure, a political naif and reactionary member of the ruling class. The purpose of Basho II is clear; he acts with knowledge and confidence in the certainty of his actions. But he no longer possesses the energy and vitality of the figure who inhabited the schematized world of parable. Instead, *The Bundle* implies a world of causes in which society has evolved disasterously; in part, because the artist has engaged the world as legislator and only secondarily as "poet." If Basho I had reflected the gap between life and art, Basho II has closed the space between action and spirit by incorporating himself into the institutionalizing process of the ruling class. While Basho I's insistence on hyperbole and detachment had fortuitously resulted in his assumption of power, his simplicity and naive self-assurance--"You get Enlightenment where you are"--had never quite implicated him in the disaster that befalls society. In *Narrow Road to the Deep North*, Basho I is manipulated by the artificial energy and forward motion of the plot. In *The Bundle*, the studied indifference of the complacent pedagogue has been refashioned. Basho II is a darkly fatalistic figure whose loyalty is bestowed on an unseen regime whose corrupt directives provide the rationale for their enforcement. Yet, as Jane Howell comments, each Basho figure seeks to retain the center of himself "in order to create--at the cost of not committing [himself] to the world--not noticing the world as it really is."[3] However, Basho's (*Narrow Road*) aperception is more the result of Bond's own indirection. In the world of *Narrow Road to the Deep North*, life resists human intervention and for Basho I implies divine intentionality; he disavows activity and remains essentially passive. Instead, he is a comic purveyor of enlightenment, a figure who dryly claims, "You can kill me of course, but it will have no importance" (p. 23), and insists with exaggerated propriety, "I don't like meddling in politics." Not fully integrated into the social hierarchy, he is neither culpable nor allowed to absorb the full responsibility for his actions. The vocation of artist and priest seem sufficiently hallowed to absolve him from any complicity. Basho implies Bond's own ambiguity, despite the author's acknowledgement of his character's guilt. Yet Bond cannot completely disavow his creation. He admits that Basho is the villain of his piece but continues, "that's a bit unfair to him, because I think if one tried to understand him a bit more, then one would have to extend one's sympathy to him too."[4]

Basho II, however, is no longer a vehicle to disperse abstractions without bearing the dramatic consequences. Perhaps Bond has resolved for himself the myth of power and its relationship to the ruling class. *Narrow Road to the Deep North* remains a parable whose comic and ironic texture indicts the artist as a sly opportunist and unwitting buffoon. Yet it is all so energetically contrived that the figure who emerges is condemned only for his passivity and lack of commitment. By *The Bundle*, Basho embodies the "myth" of the ruling class:

> The ruling class best understands the human condition, its members are the best and most intelligent of human beings and they are acting therefore only for the common good when they control and monopolize for themselves education, information, art, money, living space, medicine and everything else desirable.[5]

If the history of man implies his increasing development and subsequent alienation, Bond's socialism represents the recovery of man through himself. In the alientated world of *The Bundle*, no one, not even Basho, the representative of government and authority, experiences himself as the acting agent in his relations with the world. For Marx, as for Bond, man's relinquishment of himself is based on the distinction between existence and essence--man's existence is alientated from his essence and is not what it ought to be. Nowhere in Bond's canon is this sense of oppression more deeply felt than in *The Bundle*.

Basho, the formal artist of the play, is not only the object of Bond's enmity, he is revealed as an intermediary, alienated himself by his own capitulations. A victim of the oppression he creates, Basho, like the peasants he presides over, lacks the Bondian imagination that actuates self-appraisal: the need to examine the world, analyze its structure and alter its conditions. Though Bond creates three centers of moral interest--Wang, Basho, and the Ferryman--as he did in *Narrow Road to the Deep North*, it is through the dialectic between Wang and Basho that he draws the distinction "between fantasy on the one hand--the false inner world which people create when they have lost touch with reality--and on the other hand with imagination."[6] Basho I's failure is not that he composes worthless verse, rather his inability to realize his own humanness implies a failure of resonsibility, the result of a society which devalues the moral imagination: "the ability to imagine the feelings and the sufferings of others [that] has been restricted and withered by the culture they live in."[7]

If Bond assumes that changes in human consciousness precede changes in institutions, *The Bundle's* imaginative premise implies a shift in which the consciousness of the artist need not be restricted to artist figures. Wang, the revolutionary figure in the play, though not formally an artist, assumes the prerogatives of Bond's artist figures: a visionary imagination that enables people to see the "aspects of the situation which the socially prescribed response blots out."[8] Wang's actions possess an urgency that demand a correlative in the physical world generally authored by the Lears, Shakespeares and Clares of Bond's canon. It is not Basho who functions in the spirit of creativity or who possesses the efficacy of imagination in the play. In *The Bundle*, Bond has sufficiently demystified the artist to the extent of transferring the elements of the imagination from the exclusivity of the "artist" to a non-artistic figure. Though not precisely an artist, Wang comes closest in the play to mediating Bond's definition of the writer's function:

to enable people to comprehend their lives and to humanize society by recognizing what they must do to alter the social condition.

The implications of Bond's change in attitude are reflected in the way he reverses the opening structure of the new version. The child Basho leaves behind in the earlier play becomes a tyrant; in *The Bundle*, Wang's survival presages a new, revolutionary order. Though Basho II avidly pursues an interest in poetry and enlightenment, the fact that he remains an acquiescent candidate for a judgeship discourages our sympathy for him. When we first encounter him seeking passage on the Ferryman's raft, he is addressed as a figure who requires a deference that separates him from the society of the Ferryman and his family. From his first ceremonious utterance, the Ferryman associates him with figures of authority and repression. Basho is not, as the Ferryman guesses, a soldier or a tax collector. Yet his diction and self-conscious hyperbole suggest an air of authority as well as an obsession for self-dramatization. We suspect his complicity in a corrupt hierarchy when he archly makes pronouncements about his own worth:

> The landowner wanted to make me a judge of the fenland villages. I answered: not worthy. I have seen the darkness of human life....The truth when it is dark corrupts. First I must find enlightenment. Then I will judge.[9]

Bond hints at something specious about rhetoric that is charged with the energy of an Old Testament prophet, a dark seer whose religiosity is framed by an austere quest for purity. As a dispenser of justice and secular responsibility, his verdicts suggest a removal from the world at the behest of a visionary mysticism that is fabricated to preserve his own self-importance. His asceticism is formulated with the virtuosity of an accomplished rhetorician. The Ferryman's request for payment is artfully deflected by the poet's devotional, "For those who suffer there is grace" (p. 8). The Ferryman's further insistence is reduced by Basho's facility to formulate the right proverb at the right moment; "Does the midwife charge the child?" (p. 7), he demands of the laborer, whose only expectation had been the recovery of a meager fee. Basho neatly parries the Ferryman's request to care for the abandoned infant when he portentously announces, "Knowledge must be loved for itself" (p.8). If, perhaps, the child had been large enough to transport his bags, "...heaven's purpose," he proclaims, "would have been clear" (p. 8). The disingenuousness of his words and his own self-image--a single voice in the center of a shifting, ambiguous reality--are clarified in his formal address to the infant: "Child, I am Basho, the great seventeenth-century poet. I brought the haiku form to perfection. Listen" (pp. 8-9). He recites: "The saint's feet are hands/ Washing the dusty earth/ That leads to enlightenment/ On the Narrow road" (p. 9). The coexistence of the aspiration of the saint and the dusty earth to sanctify his ascent is a lofty projection of his own ambition. Stimulated by the echo of his own words, he assures the child "...my words are a blessing" (p. 9). As he purposefully mystifies his speech, he also takes special pleasure in a self-imposed severity and resembles an "artist" who relishes his Paris garret as a validating principle of creativity. The idea of crawling through swamps, begging, and neglecting material wants provides a self-dramatizing impulse and a source of martyrdom. More than anything else, it furnishes a portrait of the artist nourished by his own self-absorption.

When his vision is redirected to human significance, he pauses to testify briefly to the "darkness of human life--murder, theft, death" (p. 7), and surmises, "The truth when it is dark corrupts" (p. 7). Men, he implies, are opaque and unknowable--dark and elusive streams that "fret and eddy, twist into whirlpools" (p. 7). His ideology is most transparent when he counsels, like Bond's other figures of bourgeois respectability, Combe and Milton, the "long view." Bond's dialectical approach is nowhere more apparent than when the two centers of moral interest interact over the fate of the infant. M. Davis who played the Ferryman in the initial production comments that each character defines the child in terms of their own world view--the Ferryman's instinctive goodwill and the "act of grace" bestowed by Basho are two ways of perceiving the world. Basho deftly incorporates successive images of perserverence, eternity, solipsism, and the greater good in his rationale for leaving the baby behind. "Learn to be patient," he urges the Ferryman. "Would the sky alter by one tear if I took you with me? Does the ant on the mountain ask the pines why they sigh? One can take nothing into the mirror of eternity but the vision of oneself" (p. 9).

Basho is perhaps Bond's most self-conscious villain precisely because of his consciousness. The artist is finally in a position to legislate secular affairs yet his gestures remain acts of disavowal. In contrast, the Ferryman hesitates and undergoes a process of debate and internal struggle. His indecision literalizes the economic facts that generate his tentativeness and reveal the difficulty of survival. Each responds according to their status in society. Bond elaborates that

> One feels immediately that no matter how eloquently Basho talks, he is missing the point...the cleverness of his language is almost manipulating him. What he is talking about is not a true interpretation of experience but an excuse for his particular situation....When he is setting out on his journey and sees the child, he is able to refer to the child as being like an organ grinder's monkey.[10]

Yet the Ferryman's emotional commitment and implicit charity represent instances of futility, isolated gestures in a society burdened by larger insufficiencies--rational compromise fails:

> Giving way always to the immediate gesture of sympathy is not necessarily what is valuable for society....It is necessary to remove the cause of evil rather than to deal with any particular evil that crops up.[11]

Basho's return (*The Bundle*) after fourteen years of seeking is met with a recognition by the Ferryman that prompts the artist's inflated admission: "Am I known? My fame goes before me" (p. 13). Yet Bond's stage direction intimates Basho's fate: "He is old and tired and dirty. His feet are bound in lumps of rags" (p. 13). Basho's tone remains essentially unchanged; he digresses hyperbolically on crossing a "thousand valleys" on a journey that lasted "like fourteen lifetimes" (p. 13) and wearing out "seventeen walking sticks." Yet his question to the Ferryman--"...is this the way to the deep North" (p. 13)--belies his self-assurance. The realization that he fails to recognize his starting point, acknowledges that he's "walked in a circle," and confuses the Ferryman for an apparition, indicates his imperceptiveness. When he's revived, he archly pronounces the meaning of his journey: "Enlightenment! The water on my face....Enlightenment! The meaning of my journey. Heaven has shown me the mirror on my doorstep" (p. 14). As if to celebrate his new acquisition of knowledge and at the same time to conceal its essential hollowness, he poeticizes obscurely in images of reflexive mirrors, holy altars, and temples shot through with a dazzling luminosity. When Wang's inquiries about the nature of Enlightenment persist, Basho admonishes the curious fourteen-year-old and evasively "clarifies" the profundity of his experience: "I travelled the earth/ To the gateway of Heaven/ Who kept the door? Doubt!/ How many turn back/ At the last" (p. 14). His advice to Wang is formulated as a "wise" aphorism designed to undermine the youth's exhuberance: "Don't seek Enlightenment til you're ready to lose all" (p. 15). Challenged by two minor officials when he is mistaken for a poacher, Basho pontificates with verse that conceptualizes his insights as well as strategically provide the means to avoid practical commitment: "At the moment of enlightenment/ The devil springs/ What is knowledge/ Except that the world is evil?" (p. 16).

Under the tutelage of the Ferryman, Wang grows to question the assumptions and inequities of a system he barely comprehends: "We steal fish to stay alive," he tells the Ferryman, only "to pay taxes; so that there'll be no more stealing" (p. 13). The Ferryman simply responds, "We're his property [landowner]. It's in his interest to look after us" (p. 13). The climax of Wang's youth, however, occurs when he indentures himself for nine years to ensure the survival of his parents trapped on the banks of a rain-flooded river. He finally urges two scheming officials to "Buy me! Buy me! Buy me!" (p. 27). The incident typifies Bond's drama of analysis and anatomizes the inadequacy of a society to function as an agent of law and order. Wang's final words, uttered as a curse, and filled with incomprehension at his inability to control his destiny, modulate to the quiet and repose of Basho's entourage in the next scene.

Ten years have elapsed; Bond's stage directions indicate that "Basho lays his cushion on the ground, sets, unfolds his travelling desk and writes" (p. 28). It is a stunning contrast to the scene of desperation and sacrifice that we have just witnessed. Instead of his parents, it is Basho, his master, who politely confides to Wang about the affairs of men. But his experience of the world as a judge has deepened his fatalism, not altered his perception. For the first time in his canon, Bond offers the potential for utopia; an artist figure is entrusted by the ruling hierarchy to mete out justice and subsequently has the ability to shape the life of the community. Instead, Basho recounts a recent court case and casually acknowledges, "Such acts of human nature are so bestial, the time so dark that it is not possible to see what we can do to help ourselves or change the times" (p. 29). His words suggest an exclusivity that remains god-centered and self-referential. At the same time, he appropriates the Ferryman's deeds and attempts to implicate Wang in his own ethos: "You were there when I went to seek enlightenment. You were there when I found it....We call the plans of Heaven coincidence" (p. 29). Yet he remains a false mentor whose verse questions "why the poor sing." Though he formally educates his young disciple by teaching him to read, write, and study the classics, he remains a shadowy figure whose calm self-assurance belies his insensitivity. The indirection of his verse, and its conservative rejection of anything but the status quo imply a belief in human destiny that resists man's participation; the sordidness of the world, according to Basho, is the result of the intrinsic viciousness of human nature.

But it is through his poems, his artistic impulses, that we most carefully apprehend Basho's consciousness:

>   Bamboos flutter by the moorhen's nest
>   Army banners
>   She does not ask
>   Where the river goes
>   Nor where the arrow flies.
>   (p. 28)

If his first poem suggests randomness and the meandering of fate, his next poem suggests its rigidity:

>   No bird flies as fast as the arrow
>   No fruit falls as straight as the axe
>   No man escapes his end
>   Or the road to it.
>   (p. 30)

The words arrow, axe, and road imply a fixed and inflexible path on which deviation is not permitted. The words imply Basho's dogmatism; he entreats Wang to efface his past and "...stay and seek peace" (p. 30). In a temptation scene, Basho tries to seduce Wang with the prospects of the contemplative life and its accoutrements: safety, comfort and leisure. "Your hands are pale from holding a pen," he argues. "You sit by the wall while poets sing to Koto. How can you work in the fields or the shops?" (p. 29). Basho persists as a denatured artist who condemns Wang with the same fatalism he dispenses from the bench when his arguments fail. "Madmen take pleasure in destroying themselves" (p. 30), he sententiously predicts. Again, Bond uses an abandoned infant to polarize a dialectical opposition; once more a choice must be made concerning the saving of a human life. For Basho, the opportunity provides a means to seduce his young pupil. And again, he invokes providence: "Heaven has shown me a way to save you" (p. 31). Basho offers to find a place for the child if Wang will agree to remain in his household. In an example of Bond's drama of analysis (Bond uses this episode as an example in the "Preface", Wang begins to comprehend the way an oppressive social hierarchy creates a schizophrenic society using force and aggression to demean its members. The dialectic of choice presents Wang with his own dilemma of interpretation and of formalizing his relations with the world. Perhaps Bond's use of such a choice enables the audience and Wang to apprehend with absolute clarity the choice available to them. There are no ambiguities or possibilities of misperception. Bond's object is analysis, not story. Like Bond the playwright defining and defending his professional ethic, Wang's choice implies the purpose of the artist: "Moral understanding, even intellectual understanding and grasp of the situation, depends on your involvement in it. You don't stand outside..."[12] Wang's struggle, like that of his surrogate father, presents the dilemma of an essentially good man. But unlike the Ferryman, he has become conscious that isolated gestures of charity will have little bearing on the transformation of society. Perhaps he recalls Basho's personal ethic:

> I turned away from this world. I administer law for the good of heaven not the good of man. There's no help I can give to those poor so they can only seek self. They must live in ignorance..."
> (p. 30)

Bond's irony suggests that Basho's distorted sense of selfhood and his obsessive fixation with enlightenment reflect the greatest misinterpretation of events. Indeed, Wang begins to sound suspiciously like his mentor when he warns Basho prophetically, "You must leave the road from time to time--to ask if it's the right road you're on" (p. 31). But more than anything else, the episode with the infant is a testing of Wang's moral imagination. Unlike Basho, he refuses to protect and consolidate personal interests that are compatible with the landowner. Bond implies that Wang's humanism had been fostered by watching Basho mete out "justice" among the impoverished and destitute. In fact, Wang's recollection of Basho's courtroom has an eeriness reminiscent of the stories of Babel or the parables of Kafka:

> Living women with fingers twisting like ghosts, old men staring like lost children, murderers who laughed over corpses. I marveled at them as they talked: How subtle the human mind is. Each told the truth in his way, even against himself. How strange their lives, the stories of the little things that shaped them. (p. 31)

In the most decisive gesture of the play, Wang refuses to collude with a corrupt society. "How can I hold my arms wide enough to hold them all?" (p. 35), he cries and hurls the infant into the river. More aggressive and less uncertain than the Ferryman, Wang's gesture is eventually vindicated and resembles a rite of passage. Moral behavior, Bond reminds us, "depends more on social practice than on individual action. In a society structurally unjust...good deeds may in the end only support injustice."[13] Ironically, Wang's failure to repeat the Ferryman's saving act would have resulted in his own death.

Yet the commitment to revolution comes gradually. Only when he encounters a band of thieves is Wang capable of clarifying his attitude toward his former mentor. The thieves uncover a sheaf of Basho's poems and tremble before the efficacy of art; they mistake his written words for a message from the emperor and claim they rob only the poor and defenseless. But Wang's description demystifies his former master for the robbers and himself: "His hands were clean. He never raised his fist. Not even his voice. He prayed for those he sent to death. Gave money to orphans and widows. It became the meaning of ambition to follow him" (p. 43). Yet it is Wang's educated imagination joined to a moral framework that produces a play-within-a-play that interprets the world and suggests the means to redress its inequities. As a playwright and director, Wang forces the bandits to enact their own dispossession and exploitation while he explains the configuration of relations that bind them together. In the scenario, the landowner, an impoverished woman, and the river are parts Wang assigns himself and two bandits. When the river forces the woman to seek protection on the landowner's hill and he demands her possessions for his protection, the analysis becomes clear. When the flood subsides, the landowner evicts the woman and refuses to return her possessions.

> WANG.   Mine. You pay for protection.
> KAKA.   ...Why don't...the people...build a wall round the river....Then they don't need your protection.
> WANG.   Tor-quo, you are my soldier! Arrest that man.
> TOR-QUO. (goes to KAKA). Sir!
> WANG.   And hang him.
> KAKA.   Why?
> WANG.   You stole from the woman.
> KAKA.   What!
> WANG.   Her innocence.
> TIGER. Ha...
> WANG.   You see how well the landowner works. Every man must open his mouth and drink to live. He uses the means by which men live to fill them with ignorance. They live by being condemned to death. (pp. 44-45)

But Wang's creation and enactment of a common social experience is not Bond's only self-conscious use of art (role playing, much like an improvisation at a rehearsal) in the episode. Wang reads one of Basho's poems that dialectically expresses an image of Basho's own consciousness as well as the consciousness (Wang's and the theives) that he criticizes:

> The great thief
> Like little thieves
> Works in darkness
> The poor are ignorant

> They live in darkness
> What is enlightenment?
> Understanding who is the thief
> And what is the great light.
> (p. 45)

Unwittingly, Basho provides the inspiration and energy for the powers that will eventually depose him.

As Wang's revolution challenges the regime, Basho attempts to quell the unrest by encouraging the Ferryman to conspire against his son. His fatalism and inability to compromise produce familiar and deceptively logical rhetoric. Typically, his words imply the greater good: "A few will benefit by a brief happiness. A few wrongs will be righted. Anyone can do that. But those who stand the river on end, drown the coutry....Better to stop him now" (p. 48). Yet Wang's revolution necessitates the violent overthrow of the old order. The recreation of a new morality insists upon the refashioning of certain social processes because "...the government makes not only law," Wang argues, "but a morality, a way of life, what people are in their nature" (p. 59).

Fundamental to the play is the means through which such transformations might occur. "Left wing political violence," Bond argues, "is justified when it helps to create a more rational society, and when that help cannot be given in a pacific form."[14] The Ferryman finally operates as the most articulate spokesman of Wang's revolutionary politics, and emerges as its most heroic martyr. Disavowing the role of "the eyes and ears" of the emperor, he accepts the new activism and begins to ask the questions of the politically initiated: "Why are our lives wasted? We have no minds to see how we suffer. Why don't we use them to change the world?" (p. 69). The controlling image of *The Bundle*, from the image of Wang wrapped in swaddling clothes, through the "bundle" he disavows to earn his freedom, logically culminates in the image of a condemned old man splashing to the "sound of a wet bundle being hit" (p. 74).

In its final phases, the alienation that overcomes even Basho implies the sense of betrayal felt at almost every level of society: soldiers who view themselves as captives to the prisoners they guard, the water and cracker vendors who make their parasitical livelihood off peasants, the more dramatic image of a woman yoked about the head with a huge stone for stealing food, to Wang's agonized sacrifice of the infant. Even Basho's inquiry of why the retreating soldiers have provided him with no instructions in the event of an insurrection--"I expect," the commander replies, "he forgot to pass them on when he left"--implicates the landowner. Basho's final words reinforce the infidelity of the government he serves. Abandoned and betrayed, he can only utter the fact that had provided the energy for Wang's revolution: "...the government's hollow within" (p. 76). Unable to circumvent the revolution with belated pardons and dazed by the rapidity of events, Basho absent-mindedly fingers his poems while other manuscripts "slither off" the table. If the fourth scene of Part Two leaves Basho uncertain of his future--an aesthete vainly shuffling his poems--the last scene of the play constructs our final image of the artist. As the petty bourgeois and soldiers flee, and the circle of exploitation that had implicated the mercenaries, profiteers, and governor dissolves, the community that Basho helped forge disintegrates. Basho's personal fate is subsumed by the embryonic revolution and the creation of a new community. His final appearance on stage reincarnates the seeker of enlightenment in the second scene of the play; the futility and circularity of his quest are revealed in the stage directions: "He is old and weak. He clutches a few charred manuscripts. His clothes and skin are smudged with soot" (p. 80). His insensibility and the measure of his confusion is choreographed when he assaults a corpse and insists on extracting not only life, but perception from the dead: "Your face is stern....You have the way....Don't turn away....Tell me the way....The way....The way...." (p. 81). The corpse provides a resonant image of Basho in the material world; its stern face mocks the severity of his judgments, it responds coldly to his self-delusions, and it is incapable of revealing the source of enlightenment. The crafty rhetorician, reduced to child-like posturing, gropes down toward the audience, his vision marred by the fire that destroyed his house. His final words, spoken as he edges haltingly along the aisles, "I am a lost child" (p. 82), recapitulates the two infants he encountered in the course of the play. "Who will show me the way?" (p. 83) he implores. Yet even as Basho's words echo in the theatre, Wang narrates the fable of a man who never bothered to see that the figure he carried on his back had died. The incipient revolution is still in jeopardy, and the lesson that to waste one's life--"To carry the dead on your back" (p. 83), must be avoided. The broken figure of Basho is designed to discomfit, and starkly contrasts with the accidental death of a genuine revolutionary. Wang, alone on center stage, provides a reminder of the potential of any committed figure (artist or not) to alter the life of the community.

Basho's rule had been founded on his own self-sufficiency and a moribund intellectualism. Though he rationalized his way into the power structure, he is betrayed by the same system. At the conclusion of the play, his quest for enlightenment has been so deflated that his final words, "Which is the way" (p. 83), ring ironically to an audience whose primary focus is Wang, the author of the play's final words: "We live in a time of great change. It is easy to find monsters--and as easy to find heroes. To judge rightly what is good--to choose between good and evil--that is all it is to be human" (p. 83).

ENDNOTES

[1] Hay and Roberts, p. 266.

[2] Edward Bond, "A Note on Dramatic Method," in *The Bundle* (London: Eyre Methuen, 1978), p. xx.

[3] Ansorge, p. 70.

[4] Wardle, p. 9.

[5] Edward Bond, "Author's Note: On Violence," in Edward Bond, *Plays: One* (London: Eyre Methuen, 1977), p. 11.

[6] Coult, p. 71

[7] Ibid, p. 71.

[8] Edward Bond quoted in Catherine Itzin, p. 85.

[9] Edward Bond, *The Bundle* (Chicago: Dramatic Publishing Co., 1978), p. 7.

[10] Op. cit., No. 1, p. 272.

[11] Philip Roberts, "Making the Two Worlds One," *Critical Quarterly*, Vol. 21, No. 4 (1979), p. 83.

[12] *Companion*, p. 60.

[13] Op. cit., No. 12, p. 25.

[14] Edward Bond, "Author's Note," to *Saved* in *Plays: One*, pp. 16-17.

Chapter 6

PREFACE TO *LEAR* AND *THE WOMAN*

The imaginative reconstruction of history is not an uncommon feature of recent British drama; Hare's *Fanshen*, Arden and D'Arcy's *Island of the Mighty*, and Griffith's *The Party* each seek to reveal an aspect of the present by using a special insight into historical process. Like Bond's imagined histories of the lives of artists, the re-invention of characters central to the modern imagination provide the playwright with a way to reveal the pressures of the past that contain the source of our current difficulties. The stage, Lukács comments, has

> turned into the point of intersection for pairs of worlds distinct in time; the realm of drama is one where "past" and "future", "no longer" and "not yet", come together in a single moment. What we usually call "the present" in drama is the occasion of self-appraisal; from the past is born the future, which struggles free of the old and of all that stands in opposition.[1]

The aesthetic significance of mythology, Lukács contends, lies in its projection of "concrete fables" vital to our imagination and emotional life. (The lives of Lear, Achilles, and Hecuba are more real to us than their authors.) Images from the past belong to our cultural heritage yet remain sufficiently flexible to assimilate our dissatisfactions. For Bond, the conflation of past and present confronts the gap between the objective crises of society in the past (ancient Greece or Lear's regime) and a subjective response to more current issues. Instead of spiritual biographies, Bond's reworking of Shakespearean and classical texts enables him to reformulate literary history. The work of Homer, Euripides, and Shakespeare all provide the world with archetypal figures whose images imply emblems for contemporary thought and feeling. Bond's criticism, rather than the rejection of such models, represents an opportunity to revitalize productions that have failed to acknowledge the network of Tudor and Greek values that historically inform each text. The idea of refashioning historical texts for contemporary use implicitly acknowledges the inability of certain classics to pose historically meaningful perspectives.

Bond's more radical reconstruction of a text not only reconceives meaning but also calls attention to dramatic form. If, as Jacques Ehrman says, "the true subject of revolution is history,"[2] *Lear* and *The Woman* direct our attention to a social framework "in which class antagonisms were closer to the surface, economic injustice more apparent, and...the working class had not yet internalized the values of the dominant group."[3] Bond's attitude towards experience rejects a submissive acceptance of events and disregards conventional dramaturgy based on illusion and psychologically convincing characters. Instead, he explores the dynamic between individual motives and social conditions, characters determined by political realities explicated through rational analysis: "Characters in their various social roles and various social situations (and so achieving wholeness rather than developing character from its geist)"[4] define themselves in relation to one another; the audience critically considers the consequence of an action rather than the nature of the self.

Bond employs reinterpretation not as a bridge into an audience's familiar dramatic experience but as a deliberately disturbing means to undermine traditional form and to deny orthodox expectations. His departure from the privileged past in lieu of the larger focus of history provides a new totality for his dramatic purpose: to provide human beings with a new image. His symbolic versions of history repudiate certain myths that time has consecrated and legitimized--an aggressive, competitive, self-destructive society. His defamiliarizing and reordering of historical process from the "madness" of the Trojan War, to the "agrarian contentment" of *The Fool*, to the reconstituted morality of Queen Victoria and King Lear, refute the idea of reality as ahistorical and unchanging and suggest a drama of renewal and possibility. Bond's canon legitimates his claim that both life and art are subject to human intervention. Most of his plays attempt to mediate the dialectic between history and society--a dramatic lession utilized by Brecht in the *Short Organon for the Theatre*:

> The field has to be defined in historically relative terms. In other words, we must drop our habit of taking the different social structures of past periods, then stripping them of everything that makes them different; so that they all look more or less like our own, which then acquires from this process a certain air of having been there all along, in other words of permanence pure and simple. Instead we must leave them their distinguishing marks and keep their impermanence always before our eyes, so that our own period can be seen to be impermanent too.[5]

While Lear and Hecuba pursue unique destinies, they resist the function of character in conventional naturalistic drama as well as the extremity of Sartre's "theatre of situation." Sartre's drama urges "no more character," instead characters are "feedoms caught in a trap...nothing but the choice of an issue..."[6] While Sartre's dramaturgical choices seem excessive for Bond, they do essentialize the playwright's movement away from the self-referentiality of King Lear's subjectivity and Queen Hecuba's inability to act decisively. While Bond's creation of counter-texts in *Lear* and *The Woman* are designed to take the audience through the learning process of each character's life, they also provide instances in which Bond reinvents the literary past and antatomizes contemporary culture.

Bond's reenactment of historical process is evident as early as *Early Morning*; *Bingo*, *The Fool*, *Narrow Road*, *The Bundle* and *Restoration* reevaluate the forces of history by localizing contemporary issues in the past, if they do not represent a specific text. But in every instance, Bond reconsiders a past whose legacy has somehow misinformed the present. If the past is "an institution owned by society,"[7] Bond's purpose is to create a more "usable" one in order to sustain contemporary culture. Through a historical frame the audience is provided access to an aspect of events which the "socially prescribed response blots out" and so is usually hidden and distorted. Bond tells us: "I am writing about the pressures of the past that are misforming our present time, and that's where it received its public image and normative values."[8]

Rather than acts of disavowal, the action of demythologizing (a revolutionary act in itself according to Sartre)[9] examines artistically the "...expression of the need for interpretation, meaning, order--that is, for a justice that isn't fulfilled in our existing social order."[10] Yet there remains something cathartic and curative in the use of Shakespeare and Euripides to respond to the "corrupt" political process that Western society has undergone. Lear's final gesture and Hecuba's will to action provide new social contexts and insights into the process by surmounting historical limitation, conceptualizing the inequity of the political system, and finally relating them to the operation of history. No longer victims or personae in works of art that provide neither cultural nor artistic standards for contemporary leaders, each play is designed instead to aid the audience to "escape from a mythology of the past which often lives on as the culture of the present."[11] Bond's counter-mythology fashions a Queen no longer laden with suffering and a King no longer suffused with blessedness. Instead, each play resembles a prophetic text enacted for the future.

In his discussion of *The Woman*, Bond clarifies his use of Homer and Euripides to examine retroactively our own dilemmas because we

> need to set our scenes in public places where history is formed, classes clash and whole societies move. Otherwise we're not writing about the events that most affect us and shape our future.[12]

Bond's surface realism and invented past create a parable-like form in which "the quest for freedom of one man"[13] possesses an equally symbolic dimension for a contemporary audience. It is perhaps paradoxical to talk about remythification as Bond demythifies the luminous figures of posterity, fictive (Lear, Hecuba) or real (Queen Victoria, Shakespeare, John Clare, Basho). But the conflation of myth and history that Gorki ascribes to socialist realism has an equal significance for Bond:

> Myth is invention. To invent means to extract from the sum of a given reality its cardinal idea and embody it in imagery....But if to the idea extracted from the given reality we add--completing the idea by the logic of hypothesis--the desired, the possible, and thus supplement the image, we obtain the romanticism which is the basis of myth, and is highly beneficial in that it tends to provoke a revolutionary attitude to reality, an attitude that changes the world in a practical way.[14]

If one accepts E.M. Carr's argument that history is a dialogue between events of the past and the progressively emerging future, all Bond's plays, *The Woman* and *Lear* particularly, encompass that part of a dialectic that urges knowledge and action, and indicts any evasion as a disavowal of responsibility.

Rewriting the text implies human action is problematic, individuals locked in history possess the capacity to act. By selecting facts and showing the consequences of social and political behavior, Bond creates a drama of causality and choice. His reconstituted version of a classic is perhaps a drama of propaganda, but at the same time it is a drama of affirmation. Its form implies a fluid concept of the connection of art to society and suggests that the relation can change as our experience with history does. Like Brecht, Bond's drama involves a process of bringing historical events to a critical juncture in order to grasp them. Its end, like Brecht's, is a better life.

ENDNOTES

¹Lukács, pp. 426-27.

²Jacques Ehrmann, *Literature and Revolution*, quoted in Bigsby, p. 38.

³Bigsby, p. 38.

⁴Edward Bond, "On Brecht: A Letter to Peter Holland," *Theatre Quarterly*, 7, No. 30 (1978), p. 34

⁵Bertold Brecht, *A Short Organum for the Theatre*, (New York: Hill and Wang, 1974), p. 190.

⁶Jean Paul Sartre, quoted in Bigsby, p. 31.

⁷Edward Bond, "A Note on Dramatic Method," in *The Bundle* (London: Eyre Methuen, 1978), p. xiv.

⁸Christopher Innes, "Edward Bond: From Rationalism to Rhapsody," *Canadian Theatre Review*, 23 (Summer, 1979).

⁹Op. cit. No. 3, p. 38.

¹⁰Op. cit., No. 7, p. xiii.

¹¹*Companion*, p. 75.

¹²Edward Bond, "Green Room: Us, Our Drama and the National Theatre," *Plays and Players*, 26, No. 1 (October 1978), p. 8.

¹³Arthur Arnold, "Lines of Development in Bond's Play's," *Theatre Quarterly*, 2, No. 5 (1972), p. 17.

¹⁴Maxim Gorki, "Art and Myth," *Soviet Literature*, quoted in Marxism and Art, ed. Maynard Solomon (Detroit: Wayne State University Press, 1979), p. 244.

Chapter 7

LEAR AND THE RECONSTRUCTION OF TRAGEDY

> My education really consisted of one evening....We saw Donald Wolfitt in Macbeth, and for the first time in my life...I met someone who was actually talking about my problems...now I know what I have to do, what it means to be alive.[1]

What attracted Bond to *King Lear* and Shakespeare was the paradox that audiences ignore the content of the plays by calling them "transcendental;" yet they provide a set of cultural values that are central to human experience. *King Lear*, Bond notes, "...seems to deal with very fundamental desires and fears that people have."[2] Yet the myth itself, the idea that *King Lear* provides an archetypal culture figure whose standards embody a code for civilized perception supplied Bond with an artistic dilemma.

Though he insists it is among the greatest plays ever written and the one from which he derives the most insight, the Lear myth remained an obstacle to be confronted, a text to be refashioned and absorbed for contemporary use. Rather than an explicit rejection of Shakespeare's play, Bond's adaptation represents an opportunity to reclaim the play for a modern audience. "The worshipping of the play by the academic theatre," he insists, "is a totally dishonest experience. Oh, yes...this marvelous man suffering and all the rest of it..."[3] A traditional response, Bond argues, tends to treat Shakespeare as if he had the self-knowledge of modern man and fails to acknowledge the Tudor values that inform the text. The result is an invitation to intellectual laziness, and to assure the audience "Oh, how marvelously sensitive we are....You don't have to question yourself or change your society. He's a

Renaissance figure and he doesn't impinge on our society as much as he should."[4] Bond's reinterpretation implicitly acknowledges Shakespeare's inability to pose certain historical issues that at the time were barely understood. Art, for Bond, has always been prescribed by the political situation in which it is formulated, and Lear, he adds in the "Preface" to *Bingo*, is the most radical of all social critics. But Lear's insight was expressed as madness or hysteria, because at the time it was the only coherent way such perceptions could be organized.

Bond's reconstruction of *King Lear* is shaped by the playwright's preoccupation with political process: "why the classic revolution always fails." To alter society "...how do you make the revolution? That's the question...as a society you've got to answer."[5] In an unpublished essay called "Revolution," Bond recalibrates the Brecht of the *Messingkauf Dialogues*:

> To make revolution now you first have to make propaganda. It is necessary to show people the faults and the dangers of the present set-up...Unless a correct analysis is made, and is then widely understood, there won't be any change.[6]

For Brecht, theatre

> exposes any given type together with his way of behaving, so as to throw light on his social motivations, he can only be grasped if they are mastered. Individuals remain individuals but their fate becomes a social concern.[7]

Bond, like Brecht, offers us a process--political revolution in which justice implies a human form of evolution "against which is posited the institutionalized expression of authority, law, and order..."[8] *Lear* anatomizes the individual's search for freedom and rejects an interpretation of experience that glorifies the persistence of the human spirit and that imagines an apotheosis in the King's death. A.C. Bradley observes,

> If we could only see things as they are, we should see that the outward is nothing and the inward is all....Let us renounce the world, hate it, and lose it gladly. The only real thing in it is the soul with its courage, patience and devotion. And nothing can change

that."⁹

At the same time, Bond rejects Jan Kott's interpretation of an unstructured universe that is morally neutral and indifferent to the events that occur within it. Instead, he emphasizes that culture is sustained only when the perception of its members accord with the way they actualize their lives. Bond resists the idea that the source of Lear's conflict resides in the emanation of the soul. His Lear renounces passivity; his final gesture is to make revolution: "Whatever it costs, it is less than the cost of the alternative...(Lear) christens himself with revolution on the day he dies."¹⁰

Bond's dramaturgy reorganizes the idea that the playwright must divest himself of any complicity in the hero's ruin since it is not his choice, but springs irresistably from vague laws of which we possess only partial knowledge. Shakespearean design employs images of human potential (though insufficient to alter man's destiny) through a struggle in which forces superior to the individual moderate disaster by glorifying the human spirit. Bond dissociates himself from that tradition, and challenges the vision of tragedy whose locus is contemplation and wonder rather than provocation and activity. Poised against what has elusively been defined as the human spirit, Bond measures men by creative, moral dimensions, rather than depicting them trapped in the process of history, barely recognizing the direction their world is taking. It is clear that contemporary audiences rightly refuse to devalue Shakespeare's figures for their inability to comprehend history while in the process of living it, just as they don't condemn Shakespeare for not conceiving of history in the patterns of a universal historian. Bond argues, however, that such a framework embodies a dangerous passivitiy, especially from the perspective of contemporary events:

Shakespeare does arrive at an answer to the problems of his particular society, and that was the idea of total resignation, accepting what comes and discovering that a human can accept an enormous lot and survive it....What I want to say is that model is inadequate; that it just does not work. Acceptance is not enough. Anybody can accept....Shakespeare had time. He must have thought that in time certain changes would be made. But time has speeded, speeded up enormously and for us, time is running out.[11]

For theorists like Northrop Frye, tragedy is an expression of natural law which creates a web to which every act contributes. It implies a vision of the world where subjective suffering is tied to being human, and where existence itself is tragic, rather than existence modified by a deliberate or unconscious act. It particularly resists Bond's attention to particular causes and effects, the idea of historical process and that man is a rational creature capable of altering his material conditions. However, Bond's dramaturgy insists on a play of consciousness that emphasizes the idea of social utility and the act of decision-making that is more the concern of philosphers like Bruno Snell or Karl Jaspers rather than literary theorists. Snell reveals that tragedy is less interested in what occurs than in what is accomplished in terms of future ends: "...[the] essence of human action is found in the act of decision...which includes not merely the reaction to a previous fact, but also a commitment to the future."[12] Karl Jaspers defines tragic knowledge as an activity latent with the energy of choice, action and sacrifice: "...what [man] takes upon himself in the fact of which realities and in what manner of form he sacrifices his existence."[13] More a philosophy of life than literary theory, their work implicitly attempts to accommodate post-Hiroshima man rather than a figure overcome by an Aristotelian flaw in a remote and oppressive universe. More than anything else, Raymond Williams tells us, tragic experience realizes the tensions and beliefs of a culture and reflects each age's view of human experience.

In *King Lear*, the fate of the Kingdom is acted out against a backdrop of a permanence and a fixed idea of human nature. What for Shakespeare had signified an idealized relation of the sovereign, embodying and uniting his people, has for Bond become an empty ceremony. What had been an unchallenged order connecting man, the state, and the universe has become for a generation of British playwrights an abstract and depersonalized hierarchy. Bond's dilemma, which he shares with the last generation of British playwrights, is how to create contemporary tragedy extracted from the set of values and connections that no longer provide a context for it. Bond insists Lear come to terms with a finite universe whose design is embodied in man-made, artificial institutions. For modern man, the universe itself has become objective and knowable. Disorder is not rooted in the human soul, but in a system organized around the brutality and aggression that are creations of culture. The "false culture" Bond characterizes in *Lear* sustains itself by an erroneous conception of human nature.

>...if you threaten an animal so that it can't behave in a normal way, it becomes violent....And if you threaten human beings all the while, they become violent....That sort of political community we've got is based on utilizing this aggression.[14]

The structure of tragedy is embedded in a cultural source. Raymond William's remarks about the interrelation of history and tragedy find a dramatic correlative in Bond's plays and in *Lear* particularly:

>Since the French Revolution, the idea of tragedy can be seen as in different ways as a response to culture in conscious change and movement. The action of tragedy and the action of history have been consciously connected..."[15]

Not surprisingly, the Shakespearean vision of tragedy resists the idea of revolution. Though Shakespeare's tragic ethos addresses social experience, it does not question the hierarchical reordering of power or the legitimacy of authority. Yet Bond does not consciously replace Shakespearean values;

instead, his dramaturgy offers the capacity to reexamine and alter political and social experience. If tragedy suggests a time of violence and dislocation for each playwright, Bond derives a particular creativity from such crises. He reminds us that since 1917 our world has been one of successful revolution.

Lear demonstrates how violence and aggression have become institutionalized; the idea of revolution essentializes the act of rebellion and recreation. Instead of the restoration of order, even a superior one, *Lear* insists that individual consciousness can transcend a particular social function. In the process, Bond erodes the idea of a permanent human nature and the idea of absolute authority. Through Lear, he demonstrates how a single figure attempts to change the form of human activity. Lear discovers that a revolution which incorporates all the people is impossible without a change in its fundamental form of relationships.

Like his predecessor, he is a figure divested of authority and power who undergoes a process of psychic dissolution, exposure and self-recognition. Though each figure interpolates the process of pain, suffering, and perception, Bond is less interested in man's final pact with the universe than with the dialectics of aggression and the ability of the human community to sustain and regenerate itself. Each play responds to King Lear's query, "Who is it can tell me who I am?", but it is the process of Lear's education that interests Bond rather than the apprehension of "unaccommodated man." Rather, Lear becomes aware that the "world isn't there for his benefit."[16] The essential difference in the two plays lies in Lear's attempt to reinterpret and readjust his own behavior. He attempts

> to do something as a King and fails. He goes on trying to correct his failures--and it's through this attempt...that he's educated--
> -but along the way with this education...I have to show the political consequences....It's the relationship between Lear and his political activity that's interesting.[17]

Lear's passion has not diminished from its Shakespearean model, but the material and social base of his world offers a different set of solutions. What Bond derives from the mature tragedies is the spectacle of a struggle in which goodness falters, in part because government is insufficient to protect ordinary men. For Bond, "Shakespeare cannot answer his questions but he cannot stop asking them."[18] Unlike *King Lear*, who is permitted a brief moment of exaltation that sanctifies his suffering, Bond insists on demonstrating Lear's responsibility:

> ...it was very important that he could not get out of his problems by simply suffering through the consequences, or by endurance or resignation. He had to live through the consequences and struggle with them.[19]

Lear's actions and their consequences fuse a pattern of social and political action in which ideology and aspiration accord with patterns of behavior: "We must bring our daily lives with our beliefs, the economic and political basis of society in line with our ethical propoganda; we will then live in a condition of knowledge."[20] Lear's passion and energy are finally directed back to the world of men. Richard Scharine accurately remarks that what the deposed king undergoes "is no different from what many others have suffered under him. In old age he discovers the society he created by being immersed in its. His problem becomes finding a way to live in it."[21]

Shakespeare expands the conflict beyond the individual and society; King Lear pursues a settlement with a universal pattern of experience: society is insufficient to contain his stature. The disorder in his soul may be the product of social reality, but those are not the imaginative realities Shakespeare sought to investigate. Instead, he created a figure who simply overreaches the other human forces in the play. While the King's experience is rooted in social relationships, the dramatic action rapidly falls away from the rest of the dramatic personnae and centers on the King's isolation and tragic apprehension. His only recourse is to a cosmic agency that he powerlessly invokes. The implication is that death, catastrophe and recognition leave man better for his suffering, but for Bond this design evades the issue of self-scrutiny. It emphasizes the capacity to endure rather than the ability to act, and passively accepts death as the inevitable conseuqence of a fated order. While King Lear beseeches, "Is man no more than this?", Bond's ruler embodies a will to action which reflects a symptomatic response to his environment. Of course, Shakespeare's society did not bear the burden of choice that contemporary society bestows on modern man. Bond implies as much when he comments that apart from the ten major speaking roles there are approximately seventy other speaking roles that in a sense "are one role showing the character of society."[22] While Bond hypothesizes that Shakespeare hated his society because of its suffering, Lear's conflict is held in tension by social exigencies: the antagonistic demands of political and social pressure. Lear

> ...wants to have his political power and also to have his moral self-respect. The two are incompatible, because politics involves you in activities which are morally unacceptable...and so Lear becomes a critic of Lear. He becomes a critic of government, of Kingship...he attacks himself much more viciously than Cordelia or...the others.[23]

While both rulers suffer the collapse of their subjective worlds and struggle to reconstruct life on the basis of some newly acquired perception, King Lear's self-consciousness implies a membership in a broad structure that includes a higher system of nature--a moral law that operates by some investiture inherent in itself. Identity is fixed by man's place and function in that order. Absolute and intrinsically positive values confer nobility: the power of love, loyalty, compassion, generosity and family. Violation of these values are violations of nature.

For Bond, the order has become more flexible. Identity is an artifical construct created by social and political conventions and may be altered through personal assertion. Lear is capable of reshaping his identity in a finite world where design is embodied in institutions created by men, where the nature of experience has become culturally and historically conditioned. Conversely, King Lear's sheer massiveneses prevents his return to the world of his foes and supporters alike. In the imagery of the play, he is likened to a natural force: to fen sucked fogs, cataracts, hurricanes and oak-cleaving thunderbolts. Shakespeare's interests lay not simply in reconciling men but in addressing forces that exist in mystic communion with the divinity.

Yet despite Bond's transformation of *King Lear* into a poetic and political fable, Lear bears a resemblance to his predecessor. The destruction of family and the betrayal of all human relationships, the image of an incomprehensible world reduced to a play for pure power, are issues similarly bridged in each text. Perhaps each author's approach to the reality of evil and the transcendence of love, clarifies the difference in their approaches. For *King Lear*, evil is a mysterious operation poised to break loose through an error in judgment, yet it seems to have always hovered on the periphery of the king's existence. The conflict he experiences is no longer between the individual and society; the disorder in the human soul is the agent and product of the disorder in human society; its result is the inscrutable evil of Goneril and Regan and the self-destructive individualism of Lear himself. In Bond's dramaturgy, "evil" is a rational, comprehensible accumulation of the political order. Though Lear begins his dramatic life with the political opacity of King Lear, he incarnates Bond's perception that disorder results from the dysfunction of social relations in society. At the beginning of the play, he has no idea of what lies beneath the facade of the social institutions that have empowered his government. But Lear was conceived by a man who has experienced the shock of absolute evil: the devastation of World War II, Dachau, Hiroshima, Viet Nam--a world overwhelmed by a savage order of pain in which peace is short-lived, if comprehensible at all.

> *Lear* was in many ways a very grim play, and I think it's right that it should have been. I didn't want to create any false optimism, any easy optimism...because my portion of the twentieth century has been pretty stunning...and I feel that...one had to write the truth...in all its horror. But I very much wanted to maintain the feeling of strength and moral resolution, purpose in the play.[24]

The idea of the potency of human affection also joins the two plays. For King Lear, the discovery of love implies ascent and fulfillment. He renounces the world, declares his affection for Cordelia, and discerns little transcendent value except for the sanctity of his personal affections; the pain and suffering he undergoes and the recognition he is granted remain linked to that realization. In the end, King Lear is still capable of envisioning an image of an uncorrupted world; he can still experience innocence and a measure of redemption. He possesses the time to reflect:

> ...Come, let's away to prison;
> We two alone will like birds i' the cage;
> When thou dost ask me blessing I'll kneel down
> and ask of thee forgiveness; so we'll live.
> And pray o, and sing, and tell old tales, and laugh
> At gilded butterflies...
>
> (V, ii)

Lear's death is finally a release and a blessing, an implicit acknowledgement of his capacity to endure rather than to act. His withdrawal with Cordelia implies that his brief regeneration is a withdrawal from the world's turbulence--a private and personal gesture that excludes society and exalts its participants through their suffering. Love in Bond's world possesses neither the power to redeem nor the ability to establish enduring human contact. For Bond, "time is running out;" for Lear, there is no room for transcendence, no place to escape or to kneel in supplication. As if to emphasize that, King Lear's cage is an image that in *Lear* comes to delimit the idea of freedom in an age of corruption. It suggests instead the self-imprisonment of a figure entrapped by his corrupted imagination.

Part of the Lear myth reflects the inability of its principals to close the gap between action and knowledge because, as Regan surmises, each "hath ever slenderly known himself." All pretense is stripped away; life is reduced to a half-maddened old man wandering across a desolate landscape. The only basis for authenticity and human values in an inhuman environment is a recognition of mutilation. With this perception, *Lear* begins and *King Lear* gently embraces his own fall. At the end of *King Lear*, the old order is not restored so much as diminished. The King is dead and the world cannot be the same. Edgar and Albany are virtuous, but it is implied that it does not matter as much as it once did. As each voice their reluctance to ascend the throne, it becomes apparent that the new ruler will stand at the end of a historical process. Shakespearean tragedy implies a linear history and a sense of closure; *King Lear* is the drama of a single personality whose like we shall not meet again.

Bond resists the temptation to recreate the psychic history of a single personality. *King Lear* asks how to endure the unendurable in a world devoid of meaning, how to impose order and authority. Bond answers through men and their relations. Categories of good and evil exist in a complex of relations: the self is capable of mediating history, analyzing the present and determining the future. There is no Cordelia to restore Lear to a world of private feeling. King Lear essentializes these issues when he laments "is man no more than this? Consider him well. Unaccommodated man is no more than a poor fork'd animal" (III, iv). But Lear undergoes more than a process of cognition through his suffering; not only does he acknowledge the fragility of man, but he assimilates the idea of responsibility and accountability for his actions. Despite his tendency to self-dramatize his "lamentable condition," he gropes toward self-realization to the end, and in the process takes upon himself the collective guilt of society. Bond adapts the image of a single figure within a vast and uncomprehended nature and transforms the rhythm of sacrifice into a dialectical model in which one man is destroyed as others are made whole.

The process of the play is the gradual revaluation by Lear of Lear and the collapse of his project: the creation of the wall. Only when Bond's builder turns inward, only when he undergoes a process that culminates with the revaluation of his own necessity does he begin to reconstruct his life's work and transform himself. Only under the imposition of extreme stress and by grasping the repurcussions of his acts can he comprehend the limits of his creativity.

Metaphorically, the wall measures the change any figure would instigate if his project did not fulfill his expectations. In the case of *Lear*, Bond examines the attempt by the creator to rearrange and adjust his impulses, divest himself of his former biases and generate renewal. From the beginning of the play the wall implies an imposition, an unnatural obstacle whose reality suggest withdrawal and containment. It symbolizes Lear's own delusion of power and the despotism that he must necessarily impose for the preservation of "national honor" and for the "good of the people." The wall suggests one set of values at the beginning of the play and comes to reflect Lear's own growth through his perception of it. As we witness the slow and painful transformation that Lear undergoes, the wall changes hands and almost assumes an autonomous existence of its own. Though not formally a capitalist society, the world of Lear suggests a commodification of values, a centralization and brutalization of the uses of power, and a market economy aggressiveness that are each in part related to the wall or its philosophy. Political instrument and symbolic creation, the wall implies a flow of experience, which like Lear's self is never complete. As an aesthetic and literal figure, it remains one of Bond's most effective images in its conflation of freedom and restriction. The dramatic activity that surrounds the wall reflects Bond's concept of art and the function of theatre: "It has to be disruptive and questioning because at the same time it has to give a rational explanation of the circumstances in which it is occuring."[25] Lear's movement in the play, from imperceptiveness to clarity, is measured in the minds of the audience by his subjective response to the wall. Lear's self-revelation that he "must open [his] eyes and see" coincides with his final destructive gesture towards his own creation.

At the outset of the play, Lear assumes he is choosing freedom and ensuring political security through the construction of a barrier. Yet it becomes an oppressive symbol of subjugation and repressive authority. Despite his intention--"I built this wall to keep our enemies out....My wall will make you free."[26] --Lear's project is not as selfless as he claims. In the process, Lear himself becomes a parodic image of a figure who creates simply to bequeath a legacy that will glorify his memory. The wall's construction is a self-absorbed gesture, an act of solipsism that seeks to ennoble itself in a cult of personality. The emphasis in Lear's words on I and my, the subjugated you, and the preoccuption with the future tense imply basic misperceptions about his own activity. The wall provides an instrument to rationalize his own willful choices.

An iconic monument to Lear's potency, the wall also provides a means to delimit movement and restrict the mobility of his own countrymen: though it keeps intruders out, it also confines. It is the work of a politically conservative if not fascist political machine preoccupied with imaginary foes; a claustrophobic image that metaphorically chokes the people as well as providing Lear with a reflected image of his own paternity: "My enemies will not destroy my work....When I'm dead my people will live in freedom and remember my name, no venerate it" (p. 7). Yet the impulse of benevolence rapidly turns in upon itself and is refocused from an unknown enemy to his daughters when they try to censure their father---"I knew you were malicious," he denounces. "I built my wall against you as well as my other enemies" (p. 7). Subsequently, the wall impedes Lear's own feelings as well as isolating him from the world and its processes--his fixation requires his announcement of surrogates to carry out its construction at his death.

By the end of the play, the wall has clearly become an image of spiritual dishealth. The villagers talk of disease and a mad king who took the men from the village till their hands "bled for a week." Wall death, an affliction in which the worker's feet swell in the mud exudes an odor that's "like living in the grave." It is the physical correlative of Lear's compulsive energy and eventual despair. The power and theatricality of the image lies in its ordinary, physical reality and the way Bond has conflated the idea of practical activity and political reality. By the middle of the play, the wall has undermined its original intention and provides an obstacle that must be overcome. Even after Lear's deposition, the wall continues to exert and perpetuate disorder.

Yet in the social context of the play, the separation of the creator from the object of his creation is ultimately constructive and therapeutic, unlike the destructive self-division that nullifies creative activity in *Bingo* and *The Fool*. Lear's emancipation requires an act of creative deconstruction in which he emerges like Clare and Shakespeare, free and without illusions. Like Shakespeare and Clare, the intensity of Lear's vision resolves temporarily in madness. And like the delusion and apparitions the other two experience, Lear's madness signifies metaphoric doubt, and an explicit recognition of his own guilt. The self must be reformulated if Lear is to regain his sanity. The process of loss and renewal implies a recognition that his energy has been wrongly conceived. Lear's final gesture of amendment signifies emotional and political health, but also is a gesture for posterity that provides the antithesis to the legacy he originally sought to secure.

While the wall anticipates the enclosure and imprisonment of the self, the issue of freedom has its correlative in the form of Lear's madness. The ambiguity of the unfettered imagination, the flashes of insanity in Bond's canon, suggest a separation from reality; imagination no longer corresponds to reason but provides freedom and flexibility. It is precisely under these conditions that Clare, Shakespeare and Lear no longer distinguish elements of delusion from actual objects and so push beyond a conventional point of view. Madness provides a context through which characters express self-validating truths that empower them to make critical insights in the world around them. In Bond's dramatic world, madness bestows a special vision that enables its victims to penetrate the corruption of society and its institutions. In the world of the plays, it takes a particularly active and unique imagination to absorb and assimilate such truths. Such a process implies a reassessment and redefinition of one's self in relation to society and occupies a transitional phase in the life of its protagonists. The idea of entrapment employs the idea of madness and extends the concept of containment implicit in the wall into the equally visceral image of a caged animal. Lear, in his madness, creates brief fictions, abbreviated scenarios that project his own wounds and the image of a confined self: "There is a little cage of bars with an animal in it. Who shut the animal in that cage? Let it out" (p. 35). The idea of pretense is implicit in all of Lear's posturing. Bond even glosses Lear's madness as a mode of creative aspiration: "I have been a great King, now I'm going to be a great madman...in a way he acts his madness."[27] Whether real or partially feigned, Lear's madness implies a world comprised of dream, poetic vision and mystical symbols knotted by his own emotional turbulence. Madness crystalizes through intuitive gestures that fabricate elusive parables of despoliation and prophecies of a desolate future. Ironically, the corrupted imagination induces a condition of perception and employs a poetic grammar that refracts Lear's own anguish: "The night is black...and the stars are crumbs and I am a famished dog that sits on the earth and howls....My blood seeps out and they write it with a finger" (p. 17). Even the act of writing is mocked when it is interpolated into Lear's visionary insightfulness. Through such figures, he invents mythic patterns that reveal his despair in images that become more and more importunate. He dreams of a King who

> ...had a fountain in his garden. It was big as the sea. One night the fountain howled and in the morning the King went to look at it. It was red. The servants emptied it and under the sea they found a desert. They looked in the sand and there was a helmet and a sword. (p. 26)

Lear's parables embody a richly figurative language, especially when he narrates an image of his imprisoned self:

> ...an animal in a cage. I must let it out or the earth will be destroyed. There'll be great fires and the water will dry up. All the people will be burned and the wind will blow their ashes into huge columns of dust and they'll go round and round the earth for ever. (p. 37)

Images of death and violence give way to grief and knowledge that refuse to be mediated by a fictive persona. Conscious of his own mortality, Lear sadly projects himself at the center of his reverie: "I can see my life a black tree by a pool. The branches are covered with tears. The tears are shining with light. The wind blows the tears in the sky. And my tears fall down on me" (p. 86). Comprehension implies sight and renewal; Lear reasserts himself in almost classical terms: "I must walk through my life step by step. I must walk in weariness and bitterness....I must open my eyes and see" (p. 60). The act implies not merely cognition but recognition. When he prostrates himself by the wall he constructed, his act of renunciation dissolves in a gesture of supplication: "I kneel by the wall. How many lives have I ended here?" (p. 66). For the remainder of the play, Lear hopes to create with a new sense of possibility. Despite the censure of Cordelia's regime--"...you will not speak in public or involve yourself in any public affairs" (p. 78), Lear refuses to be stilled; his final admonition addresses Cordelia's perception of sight rather than her political wisdom. His only recourse is to act destructively, but the act is nonetheless achieved with a political consciousness. His words emphasize the need to act, but in a context of struggle that addresses the limitations of all repressive regimes: "What can I do? ...still I'm a prisoner. I hit my head against a wall all the time. There's a wall everywhere. I'm buried alive in a wall" (p. 80).

It is in this frame of mind that Lear utters his last parable, a sermon to the disaffected that metaphorically reveals an approach to creativity and the political consequences of a life of art. From the image of a denatured animal that mocks the creative act, to a vision of devastation and the imprisoned imagination, Lear speaks of a man who "...found he'd lost his voice. So he went to look for it, and when he came to the woods there was the bird who'd stolen it" (pp. 74-75). Like the man whose search for articulation leads him to imprison a singing bird, Lear's search for his self results in a process of suffering and recognition. The bird's feathers are pulled out by the authorities because it insists on singing the truth despite the King's admonitions. It is a negative fairy tale that, like Buchner's, ends badly with the man "stamping his feet...locked up for the rest of his life in a cage" (p. 75). Yet his voice re-echoes in the forest because "the bird had the man's voice" and kept singing and "soon the other birds learned it" and were singing in the woods. Perhaps the process of the story, the politicized fable, is Lear's greatest creation. Uttered in peace and comprehension, it remains an act of rebellion, an antidote to the creation of the wall.

More than any other of Bond's dramatic figures, Lear's movement implies the furthest distance explored, the greatest knowledge acquired. From solipsism to engagement, from silence to skepticism, his final gesture, despite its scale, is designed to exert pressure on the social order. Through the process of his dialectic--"We develop through our problems, not just solving them, but through clashing with them."[28] Bond constructs a "method of change":

> I have not answered many of the questions I have raised, but I have tried to explain things that often go unnoticed but which must be right if anything is to work for us....There is no need for pessimism or resignation, and this play is certainly not either of these things. I have not tried to say what the future should be like, because that is a mistake. We do not need a plan of the future, we need a method of change.[29]

In order to analyze Bond's strategy more thoroughly, I have examined in detail the process of such a method.

Act One occupies an invented landscape that suggests contemporary references as well as a mythic past. The play is full of anachronisms that connect Lear's political choices with their modern counterparts. In William Gaskill's production, Lear and his daughters resemble the royal family, happily on their way to visit a shipyard. Yet Lear's first act is to personally execute a workman because it interferes with what has become his lifelong obsession, the creation of the wall: "I started this wall when I was young. I stopped my enemies in the field....How could we ever be free?" (pp. 3-4). In his "Preface," Bond asserts that, "Act One shows a world dominated by myth."[30] Part of this structure implies that metaphoric walls are necessary to maintain peace and to protect Lear's constituency. The idea of a despot whose benign goodwill imposes a moral structure on his kingdom through the sheer magnitude of his rhetoric is also a myth that Bond has in part derived from Shakespearean precedent. Driven by personal necessity rather than by any sense of justice, Lear ruthlessly orders a man shot because he ostensibly conspired to delay work on the wall. The way Lear fails to recognize his own complcity in the first place implies the equivocation with which he addresses his daughters and rationalizes his own messianic complex. Lear glorifies his ambition and misinterprets the shrewdness of his daughters as they protest his cruelty. His language is rhetorical and conceived in self-interest; there is barely the intention of genuine communication: "You're too good for the world...you're right to be kind and merciful, and when I'm dead you can be....Only I'm not free to be kind and merciful" (pp. 4-5). Lear's paternalism sustains the myth of a legacy that he will bestow on the future and the idea of offspring who exist to gratify his conception of them. But the preservation of a corrupt order that arrogates human necessity to the erection of barriers and allots punishment in return for anything less than obedience is a position Lear will retreat from by the end of the play. Like Shakespeare in *Bingo*, Lear recants the myth of his own absolute authority when he accuses the Counselor near the end of the play: "You good, decent, honest, upright men who believe in order---when the last man dies, you will have killed him" (p. 79).

The process of the play accounts for the way Lear is disabused of the myth of a self he has meticulously constructed; his misuse of power and authority implicates him in the destruction of the kingdom and the death of innocent men. It is precisely the myth of power and its abuses that Bond addresses when he argues in the "Preface," "It's so easy to subordinate justice to power, but when this happens power takes on the dynamics and dialectics of aggression..." (xiii). The revolution inspired by his own rashness, the revolt of his daughters and the elaboration of the ideology of his regime in the subsequent insurgency of Cordelia, recreate elements of his most destructive policies. The innocence and reasonableness of his daughters' protestations--"Father, if you kill this man it will be an injustice" (p. 4), and their pleas to the soldiers--"If the King will not act reasonably, it's your legal duty to disobey him" (p. 6)--belie their macabre behavior after they assume power. Their incredulity at the injustice they witness in terms of their later actions suggests a division of experience that originates in Lear's self-serving and empty slogans about "protection," "loyalty," and the "good of the people." When Lear rages against the possibility of their marriage, he implicitly indicates the retributive role they will represent. He reveals his position in the cycle of violence when he execrates (against the prospective grooms), "They're my sworn enemies. I killed the fathers, therefore the sons must hate me" (p. 5). Bodice's callow idealism, "...how can they be your friends if you treat them like enemies? That's why they threatened you: it was political necessity" (p. 5), prepares the audience for the difference in the two sisters after they acquire power and are transformed into guignol figures of farce. Even as his daughters instigate the revolution that will depose him, Lear's concern is divested of human concerns and becomes instead, an extension of his obsessive ego. The horror he recounts--"Armies on their hands and knees in blood, insane women feeding children at their empty breasts, dying men spitting blood..." (p. 7)--creates a vision of apocalyptic horror and the perversion of civilized conduct. Lear envisions a world in ruins, created by his own destructive policies and historical precedent. Perhaps the greatest myth of the first act is Lear's illusion that upon his death, "people will remember my name and live in freedom and peace" (p. 7). Essentially, Lear's existence has been structured around a series of fabricated self-deceits. His recognition of his role in the retributive cycle will be won painfully, only after great hardship.

Because he is interested in political process, especially the mechanism of revolution, Bond comments in the "Preface," "I begin at the revolution."[31] Lear is overthrown and the campaign he unsuccessfully wages to recover his kingdom bears a ludicrous resemblance to the trappings of military heroism at the beginning of World War I; Lear clicks his heels and in the best military tradition salutes his gallant and glorious command. As he assembles an archaic plan of battle, he gathers around him all the figureheads of a corrupt command and a bureaucratic system: a Bishop to bless his encounter with the enemy, the Counsellor to support the righteousness of his cause, and a loyal but insensate military man. Yet he still finds it impossible to grasp his daughters' motives and ironically inquires, "Where does their vileness come from?" (p. 9). The mutilation of Warrington, the intrigue of each daughter to betray and usurp the other, and Lear's gestures of incomprehension and self-pity, demystify the myth of battle that instead dissolves in military adventurism.

Defeated and alone, taunted by visions of his daughters, the image of the disfigured Warrington provides a reflection of his own condition: "He's dead. I saw his face. It was like a stone" (p. 22). Bond provides Lear with just enough awareness to acknowledge the shock without being capable of reflecting on its origin. He is aware of the misery of his own existence without being able to isolate its causes. When he stumbles upon the Gravedigger Boy's pastoral way of life he can only wonder, "I should have spent my life here....It's so simple and easy" (p. 25). Lear absolves himself from the consequences of his regime except for matters that might alter his immediate condition: "Where shall I go, How can I live, What will become of me?" (p. 25). Unknowingly, he brings the corruption of the Kingdom to the pastoral life of the Boy; but his appearance provides the source of taintedness that will destroy his temporary haven. In what seems like a world of prelapsarian simplicity, Lear seeks to mediate the tragedy of his existence by dismissing the past, diminishing his own culpability, and beginning again: "I could have a new life here. I could forget all the things that frighten me--the years wasted on my enemies, my anger, my mistakes" (p. 25). Yet it is precisely the burden of the past and Lear's attempt to efface its memory that Bond dramatizes. He refuses to permit Lear any release or escape. The body of Warrington that stains the Boy's well prefigures Lear's own pollution and foreshadows the pillage and destruction of the farm-like sanctuary. Despite Lear's request to spare the farm and his voluntary surrender, the murder of the Boy and the rape of his wife suggest a surrogate sacrifice, just as Warrington replaced Lear as the object of his daughter's rage. By the end of the act, there is little honor or glory, only Lear's imprecations: "...burn the house. You've murdered the husband, slaughtered the cattle, raped the mother, killed the child, you must burn the house. You're soldiers, do your duty" (pp. 30-31). Lear's final words recreate the exhortations that began the first act, but now are uttered under the pressure of personal calamity. The parodic violence done to Warrington by the sisters dissolves in the vicious destruction of the farm and its inhabitants. As Lear implies in his final words, the act of violence has become a normative process. One critic comments that having gone through all King Lear suffered in the first act, Bond's Lear learns nothing at all. But that is precisely Bond's intention. Though he does not yet permit Lear to grasp the shape and design of events, he at least permits him to perceive and acknowledge their repercussions.

In Act Two, the process of education continues. Every time Lear "gets closer to the truth, he thinks he knows the whole truth."[32] On trial and condemned by his daughters, Lear is prosecuted by the system he instituted. The judge he empowered and the Counsellor he employed deny his rights because they are motivated by self-interest. Images of casual betrayal and corruption, of specialized political officers and brutal interrogations pursue Lear despite his admission of complicity. Bond describes the act as demonstrating the clash between myth and reality--a movement that implies the beginning of Lear's self-realization and recovery. Traumatized by the events of the past six months, Lear gazes into a mirror and exclaims, "...that's not the King. This is a little cage of bars with an animal in it. Who shut the animal in the cage--let it out....O God there's no pity in this world" (p. 35). The denatured world finds its fulfillment in the image of a caged and broken animal. The emotional turbulence of the animal, one critic suggests, reflects what the suffering King Lear undergoes on the heath. The pathos of suffering prompts Lear's own identification with the animal and the tortured utterance, "I can't live with the suffering in the world" (p. 35). It is the first acknowledgement of a complex of events that Lear helped to preserve. Yet the emphasis syntactically remains on the obsessive "I". Lear continues to be the center of his own universe; the condition of society remains external to the satisfaction of his own needs. Imprisoned, he seeks only to nullilfy what he is forced to concede for the first time. "It is too unbearable," and "I must forget," are impulses of a man who has not yet recognized the suffering that binds men in an oppressive society. The trapped animal of Lear's imagination reflects his unrest; it attempts to pry into Lear's consciousness, to uncover the past, and prophesizes the future. It exacts recognition that is devastating: "I killed so many people and never looked at one of their faces....Wrong. Wrong. Wrong" (p. 42).

Lear's education evolves when the Ghost of the Gravedigger's Body conjures up the spirits of his executed daughters. As young girls, they perch on Lear's knees and suggest innocence uncorrupted by their father's duplicity. Part of the education Lear undergoes is the recognition that his daughters had been shaped by his activity, children of his state for whom he bore reponsibility. In the only domestic scene of the play, Lear tenderly strokes their hair, cradles them affectionately, and rhapsodizes about a world that might have been. It is a powerful theatrical image that gains its effectiveness from the audience's memory of the grotesque figures of the second act. Finally capable of recognizing the suffering around him, Lear resists reflecting on its origin and production. Instead of addressing the need to alter the circumstances in which he finds himself, he seeks refuge in gentle stoicism: "I know it will end. Everything passes, even the waste" (p. 39). Such understanding suggests partial knowledge, but remains an awareness that resolves itself in an image of Sophoclean acceptance. The fact that Lear admits, "I can't live with the suffering in the world" (p. 35), reminds us he remains unchanged.

Cordelia, more Lear's spiritual heir than his daughters, provides the context for the counter-insurgents. Her politics, like Lear's, are generated by an elitism that issues in disastrous consequences for the creation of community. A captured soldier is executed because he doesn't hate sufficently. "To fight like us you must hate," she explains to the Carpenter, "you can't trust a man unless he hates" (p. 44). Her ideology is a rationalized reassertion of Lear's theory of power, which she promptly justifies: "When we have power these things won't be necessary" (p. 45). Cordelia is Bond's unsuccessful Robespierre:

> Lenin said we must have this elitest section to lead the party, because the proletariat just doesn't have enough consciousness to know what's going on...when Lenin died, Stalin could simply carry on--when you have an elite, you have to destroy the proletariat in the same way.[33]

If Cordelia aspires to the reordering of the political process, Lear's daughters represent a diminution of even Lear's sense of order. During their brief regime, spies become "the only moral institution in the country" (p. 46). The pressure of power entangles the politically naive in such an impossible series of events that their intrinsic selves are distorted. Bodice admits, "My decisions are forced upon me. I change people's lives and things get done--it's like a mountain started moving forward, but it's not because I tell it to--I'm trapped" (p. 48). The image of entrapment and loneliness of the caged animal is vaguely intuited by the sisters; power is an obligation Bodice is almost forced into against her will: "Now I have all the power...and I'm a slave" (p. 49), she cries disconsolately.

At the same time, Lear is full of gentle paternalism; he concedes to the Ghost he "did him a great wrong once" (p. 54). Yet his serenity belies the urgency for change if community is to transcend mere functionalism. As the Ghost decays, Lear apprehends more; but his guilt and need to harbor the Ghost is directed toward the past, an impulse designed to protect his own heritage. Lear's guilt is clearer when Fontanelle denounces her father: "For as long as I can remember there was misery and suffering wherever you were....You've wasted my life and I can't even tell you" (p. 56). Bond's purpose is clear as Lear slips into madness:

> Some things were lost to us long ago as a species, but we all seem
> to have to live through part of the act of losing them. We have to
> learn to do this without guilt or rancour or callousness--or social-
> ized morality.[34]

The Ghost persists as Lear's tempter, an image of remembrance that offers easy escape: "I'll take you away. We'll go to the place were I was lost" (p. 50). But Lear remains inflexible: "...I ran away so often, but my life was ruined just the same. Now I'll stay" (p. 58). The process reaches a temporary resolution when the former King witnesses the autopsy performed on his daughter. Bond recalls King Lear's figurative language: "Then let them anatomize Regan, see what breed's her heart" (IV, v), when Lear gazes at Bodice's remains. His rage dissolves in wonder:

> She sleeps like a lion and a lamb and a child. The things are so
> beautiful. I am astonished. I have never seen anything so beauti-
> ful....If I had known she was so beautiful....If I had known this
> beauty and patience and care, how I would have loved her. Did I
> make this and destroy it? (p. 59)

Unlike Shakespeare's vision of transcendent evil existing of and for itself, Bond crystalizes the idea that no cause in nature is sufficient to make Fontanelle's heart hard. Lear acquires a reverence for uncorrupted creation--the biological birthright every individual inherently possesses. But it is his own dereliction of responsibility that he must acknowledge before he can evolve further.

> I knew nothing, saw nothing, learned nothing. Fool, Fool....And now
> I must begin again, I must walk through my life step by step, I must
> walk in weariness and bitterness. I must become a child....I must
> open my eyes and see. (p. 60)

Bond dramatizes the acquisition of insight by blinding Lear in a way that suggests the crisp efficiency of modern technology. His scientist/captor is polite, breezily efficient and without feeling. Violence is officially sanctioned and has become as much a part of public policy as Lear's legalized executions at the wall. Blind and powerless, Lear still refuses the Ghost's entreaties. "Surely you have suffered enough" (p. 64), he beseeches Lear. The Ghost urges limitation and isolation, and bearing pain in silent stoicism. However, Cordelia has resumed construction on the wall, and when Lear encounters a family about to enlist their son in her service, he prostrates himself at the foot of the battlement and urges the boy to flee. Stricken with an image of his own creation, Lear and the audience are forced to consider the scope of human suffering: "All life seeks safety. A wolf, a fox, a horse--they'd run away, they're sane. Why do you run to meet your butchers?" (p. 56). With only the Ghost as his companion, he laments: "Men destroy themselves and say it's their duty. How can they be so abused?" (p. 67).

In Act Three, the past is no longer tenable. Even its memory is incompatible with the present; Lear begins to address the world of political necessity. Bond tells us that

> Lear is tempted with visions of the past age because it represents a naive simplicity, a happier time. But that's a destructive attitude--you can't return to the past. People who talk about the past as a golden age are usually the most dangerous, like the Nazis, for example; Lear has to reject that sort of conception.[35]

As a political dissident, he discounts Thomas's fear that his generosity will lead to a condition in which "...we'll all be responsible" (p. 73). Lear's pacifism suggests responsibility, but at the same time Thomas expresses Bond's belief that words themselves are insufficient.

> We talk to people but we don't really help them. We shouldn't let them come here if that's all we can do. It's dangerous to tell the truth. The truth without power is always dangerous. And we should fight. Freedom's not an idea, it's a passion. (p. 76)

Thomas's activism finds a spokesman when Lear's former Counsellor confronts the deposed monarch and demands that he recant. Lear's response is an act of expiation; he assails the self-justifying principles of a regime that supplanted his own. Yet he still denies the efficacy of action when he laments his own powerlessness: "What can I do? I left my prison, pulled it down, broke the key and still I'm a prisoner....Does this suffering and misery last forever?....I can do nothing, I am nothing" (p. 80).

The Ghost, attenuated and importunate, counsels submission and exhorts Lear to send the supplicants away: "Let them learn to bear their own suffering....That's the world we have to learn to live in. Learn it" (pp. 80-81) But Lear's final words to the Ghost are decisive, "They're coming to bury me and I'm still asking how to live" (p. 82), and prepare us for his confrontation with Cordelia. In recreating the myth, Bond's purpose, in part, was to "redefine the relation between Lear and Cordelia....Cordelia in Shakespeare's play is an absolute menace...she's a very dangerous type person."[36] Her idealism, a critic points out, derives from a savior complex, but her motives obliquely suggest Lear's formative influence and punctuate the short deadly reign of his daughters: "...your daughters were killed. And it's clear there's no real difference between you and them." Lear replies, "None" (p. 83). His admission, one of the central truths of the play is uttered at great personal cost and implies the degree of his political maturation. But Cordelia's insistence that her revolution is "creating new life--you must stop speaking against it" (p. 83), is a partial admission that Lear speaks as the sublimated voice of her own uncertainties. When she refuses to halt construction of the wall at Lear's behest, he sadly admits that nothing has changed. "A revolution must at least reform" (p. 84), he pleads. "If you create a violent revolution, you will always create a reaction," Bond explains. "Lenin thinks, for example, he can use violence for specific ends. He does not understand that he will produce Stalin..."[37] Yet Lear's words still suggest withdrawal and the passive wisdom associated with the aged Tolstoy or *Oedipus at Colonnus*:

>I suffered so much, I made all the mistakes in the world and I pay for each of them...You have two enemies, lies and the truth...you sacrifice truth to destroy lies and you sacrifice life to destroy death. It isn't sane....Our lives are awkward and fragile and we have only one thing to keep us sane; pity, and the man without pity is mad. (p. 84)

Cordelia chooses to refute his arguments with political slogans: "...we'll make the society you dream of" (p. 85), but Lear's final words--"Your law always does more harm than crime and your morality is a form of violence" (p. 85)--reemphasize the words of the "Preface": "Aggression has become moralized, and morality has become a form of violence,"[38] and remain Lear's most acute recognition of the structure of society. The Ghost's "death" dramatizes the end of any commitment to the ideals of the past, and Lear, as if to divest himself from his former persona, admits "It's too late....You were killed long ago....You must die...for your own sake" (p. 86). In Lear's search for self-value, the Ghost must be disowned. In Gaskill's production, the Ghost appeared whenever Lear wants to escape from reality and reason. As Lear disavows the burden of the past, he finds himself at the foot of the wall:

>LEAR. I'm not as fit as I was. (He digs up
>a shovel of earth. The Farmer's Son, whom
>earlier Lear tried to save, aims his pistol.)
>
>>But I can still make my mark.
>
>(The Farmer's Son fires. Lear is winged...
>he spits on his hands and grips the shovel.)
>
>>One more.
>
>(He scrapes more earth down. The Farmer's Son
>aims, fires, and hits. Lear is killed instantly
>and falls down the wall. Some of the workers
>move towards the body with curiosity...The
>workers go quickly and orderly. One of them
>looks back.)
>
>(pp. 87-88)

Lear's final movement is an act born of expiation; it implies the process of growth and cautious optimism. The worker's glance back fuses the destiny of the dead monarch, if only for an instant, and if only in death, with the interest of the collective. Lear's disavowal is an act of reassessment that insists that history will not repeat itself. His life concludes as he sets an example to the young people who remain: "They are the really important people in the play--they represent...a new possibility for change in society. They are my equivalent to Fortinbras."[39]

In the final stage of the play, Lear's status as a living image of resistance has given way to a symbol of political dissidence. Though Bond will repudiate his skepticism about the efficacy of violence to accomplish a revolutionary purpose in *The Bundle*, Lear's final gesture remains undiminished. His transgression, his "One more" is a "gesture beyond"; as Ruby Cohn notes, "Lear will not be the last rebel--there will always be the possibility of one more."[40]

ENDNOTES

[1] Edward Bond, "Drama and the Dialectics of Violence," *Theatre Quarterly*, 2, No. 5 (January-March 1971), pp. 5-6.

[2] Glen Loney, "Interview with Edward Bond," *Performing Arts Journal*, 1, No. 2 (Fall 1976), p. 40.

[3] *Gambit*, p. 24.

[4] Ibid.

[5] John Hall, "Edward Bond," *The Guardian*, 29 (September 1971), p. 10.

[6] Hay and Roberts, p. 106.

[7] Bertold Brecht, *Messingkauf Dialogues*, quoted in Hay and Roberts, p. 118.

[8] Op. cit., No. 6, p. 107.

[9] A.C. Bradley, *Shakespearean Tragedy* (Greenwich, CT: Fawcett, 1965), pp. 270-271.

[10] Itzin, p. 78.

[11] Op. cit., No. 5, p. 10.

[12] Bruno Snell, *The Discovery of Mind*, trans. T.G. Rosenmeyer (Cambridge, MA: Harvard University Press, 1953) pp. 106-107.

[13] Karl Jaspers, *Tragedy is Not Enough*, trans. K.W. Deutsch (London: Victor Gollary, 1952), p. 56.

[14] Op. cit., No. 1, p. 8.

[15] Raymond Williams, *Modern Tragedy*, p. 73.

[16] Op. cit, No. 3, p. 24.

[17] Op. cit, No. 6, pp. 112-113.

[18] Edward Bond, "The Rational Theatre," *Plays: Two*, p. x.

[19] Op. cit., No. 1, p. 9.

[20] *Companion*, p. 52.

[21] Scharine, pp. 216-217.

[22] Edward Bond, *Lear* (London: Methuen, 1972), pp. 2-3.

[23] Op. cit., No. 2, p. 41.

[24] Op. cit., No. 6. pp. 137-138.

[25] Op. cit., No. 3, p. 5.

[26] Op. cit., No. 22, pp. 2-3.

[27] Op. cit., No. 6, p. 123.

[28] Hugh Herbert, "Edward Bond," *The Guardian*, (4 August, 1974), p. 10.

[29] Op. cit., No. 22, p. 11.

[30] Ibid., p. 12.

[31] Op. cit., No. 3, p. 25.

[32] Perry Nodleman, "Beyond Politics in Bond's *Lear*," *Modern Drama*, 23, p. 272.

[33] Op. cit., No. 1, p. 9.

[34] Ibid.

[35] Matherne and Maiorana, p. 68.

[36] Op. cit., No. 1, p. 8.

[37] Op. cit., No. 5, p. 10

[38] Op. cit., No. 22, p. 5.

[39] Op. cit., No. 6, p. 137.

[40] Ruby Cohn, *Modern Shakespearean Offshoots* (Princeton: Princeton University Press, 1976), p. 66.

Chapter 8
THE WOMAN AND SEXUAL POLITICS

Edward Bond's reassessment of the way historical process intersects the lives of artists and literary figures--Shakespeare, Lear, John Clare, and Basho--matures in *The Woman*, a play he concedes summarizes his previous concerns and sets them in a framework borrowed from the classical past. If the theatre can assess and evaluate human nature, the process is glorified in plays like *King Lear* and *The Trojan Women*. "I've been inspired," he acknowledges, "by Shakespeare and Euripides...and Chekhov."[1] If *The Woman* employs a number of archetypal myths from the classical tradition, Bond's demythologizing of the idea of a Heroic Age sustains his most exhaustive exploration of the self-defeating antagonism of an irrational culture.

In the "Preface" to the play Bond admits that "...the world will always be a place of...some difficulty and...of loss. This does not mean that it will destroy us or that we must destroy it and ourselves."[2] If we possess a moral obligation to acknowledge that every action has political consequences, *The Woman* represents a muted possibility that recognizes loss but aspires to the future. Subtitled *Scenes of War and Freedom*, the play addresses the issues of *Saved* and *Lear* but finally modulates to an affirmation of human life and rationality that proves itself. If the world of *The Woman* reforges the classical past and the heroic world of Homer, it does so with a particular incentive: to explore our investment in the past and how it relates to our present condition. Bond tells us that

> It isn't a play about the past. It's a play about the present. Greek society created us. We live in the world of the Greeks. We don't have the problems of recreating the past, we have the more difficult problem of creating the present.³

As a precondition to writing, Bond travelled to Malta "...to face the sun on the rocks,"⁴ and re-read all the extant Greek tragedies and comedies. While the influence of Euripides is perhaps more evident, Bond's treatment of classical civilization implies a familiarity with the *Iliad* and its heroic conventions, if only to deflate and poise them ironically against the values of our own society.

In Bond's treatment, the Greek forces led by a general-statesman, Heros, lay siege to Troy in order to recover an elusive female; but it is not the fabled Helen of classical myth. In a parodic version of the image of beauty that captivates men's imagination, the object of the assault is a stone image of the Goddess of Fortune, an icon whose possession in the patterning of the action is necessary to ensure military success and political viability. That the image, "a plain schematized female shape of a woman, but not smooth stone, about three-quarter size" (p. 49), seems nondescript belies its figurative function in the texture of the play. A religious symbol, an image of power and a fetishistic correlative to man's obsessiveness, the statue's acquisition ultimately resolves in the destruction of Heros as well as the Trojan forces. It stands at the outermost ring of a series of three female figures that collectively reflect the image of the woman of the play's title.

Bond explores the crises in the ancient world as a polarized tension between male and female prerogatives. The issue of gender and the antagonism associated with male and femaleness organizes the play's values and its sexual politics. Though it is a simplification to imply that Bond imputes the values of force and aggressiveness to the males and compassion and reconciliation to the women, the antagonism between male and female modes of perception informs the play's organization. Bond discloses that he sought to clarify his own biases by looking

> ...at the world from the point of view of women. Not because they are inhabiting a different world, but because it enabled me to get away from my own sexist prejudices by trying to put all the moral responsibility, all the moral development into the character of the women.[5]

The Woman provides an instance in which the idea of patriarchy--a mode of power relationship and male domination instigated through ideology and institutionalization dissolves under its own weight. The action of the play provides an index of humanization, a celebration of humanness over brutality that dramatizes the perceptions of Charles Fourier, quoted approvingly by Marx in *The Holy Family*:

> The change in a historical epoch can alway be determined by the progress of women towards freedom, because in the relation of woman to man, of the weak to the strong, the victory of human nature over brutality is most evident. The degree of emancipation of women is the natural measure of general emancipation[6]

Bond treats the female figures in the plays as individuals capable of comprehending and resolving the same moral and political issues as men. In fact, the only figures capable of grasping the events with imaginative clarity are Hecuba, Queen of Troy, and Ismene, whose maturation from Hero's decorous wife to radical dissenter provides the impetus for the first half of the action.

When Hecuba first insists on privately talking to Ismene--"Perhaps two women could find some way of solving this," (p. 28)--Thersites, leader of the Greek delegation, responds that "Wars are not decided by women talking" (p. 28). Equally suspicious, and a reflection of the Trojan-Athenian tensions, the two women grope twoards some form of communication. Ismene vaguely denies Hecuba's accusation that "We both know the truth: your husband would take the statue and still burn and kill and loot" (p. 33). But Ismene's idealism provides the possibility of a solution when she refuses to return to the Greek camp and remains in Troy as a willing hostage. Her instinctive attempt to mediate the hostility through legitimate negotiation reveals the Greek duplicity. Thersites glosses the Athenian "art" of diplomacy when he corrects Ismene's precipitous gesture. It is her first political lesson: "In politics you always ask for more. If we agree to this what will they want next?" (p. 35). Heros is humiliated at the prospect of coming home "...with a statue and no wife" (p. 35), and is especially distressed at the thought of being outmaneuvered. In what seems like a male conspiracy, Hecuba's son deposes his mother and declares with typical male bravado, "I have faith to inspire the people" (p. 39). Ismene's naiveté and facile idealism can hardly cope with the politics of an irrational society;

> How well everything's worked out. The Trojans will give the Greeks what they want: the statue. And the Greeks will do what the Trojans want: go. And when they do I'll follow. (pp. 36-37)

Her hopes are betrayed when the Son assumes power and admonishes "...the war starts now" (p. 36). Ismene and Hecuba, allied by their imprisonment, are similarly betrayed by male prerogatives. Each watches with increased anxiety as events unfold beyond their control. Ismene confesses that her husband had deceived her and achieves a new independence when she calls down to the Greeks from the Trojan battlements: "Go home....You're wasting your life making your tombstone! No one answered: there is no answer" (p. 43). Yet an answer occurs to her: "If they lose Athens will throw them out" (p. 44). Hecuba sits, watches, and acknowledges, "I saw this war corrupt almost everyone it touched. It's taken you to the limit of corruption" (p. 47). Tried for treason by the Greeks, Ismene is diagnosed as "defiant," her "insanity" produced by undue stress. The male court defends itself by charging that "they'd do the same to us," and "our men are entitled to their day" (p. 50). But the trial does furnish Ismene with an opportunity to articulate what she has learned:

> In Troy I saw the people suffer. Young men crippled or killed, their parents in despair or dying of disease. I told them as they were dying--I shall do all I can to stop this. No more suffering caused by men." (pp. 54-55)

Finally, Ismene has learned to ask the right questions; her words are addressed more to the audience than to a mock jury of Greek militarists: "Many people die saying what I've said. Who are they? Who killed them? How many will die and who'll know?" (pp. 54-55). Bond argues that her indictment is

> ...an appeal against the waging of the war, which is a humanist appeal; that is, Ismene takes the line--it's all she can do--that if she appeals to people's reason, that will have some effect.... she says she believes that the world is fundamentally a rational place and therefore simply to record the truth is a valuable thing because it becomes part of the experience of other people and changes them. What she does is more than just make an appeal; she does affirm a belief in the values of faith and understanding and reason.[7]

Harold Hobson perceptively explains, "It's not a woman who causes the Trojan War, but it is women who try to stop it."[8]

If Homer's epic sought to create a world where men resembled gods through a stylized ritual of combat in order to commemorate themselves to posterity, *The Woman* returns its personae to a more familiar landscape of avid militarists, conquest and the sanctified idea of homeland; each implies the devaluation of human life. Bond returns to the past in order to

> ...reexamine that world and how moral and rational it was, and whether...it could be a valid example for a society like ours. I came to the conclusion that it wasn't....I had to...reverse those values so...there is a man, Heros, who stands for the classical values of beauty and order, and he is opposed by a miner who stands for a new order, for a new proletarian direction of history.[9]

Homer's philosophic and aesthetic framework, however, was not designed to reveal the inadequacy of a class structure but to mythify the past. *The Woman* eclipses the Homeric preoccupation with honor and virtuosity: instead the bravura feats of Hector's heroism dissolve in Heros' cool suavity and brazen ambition. Facile diplomacy and a brutal insensitivity to human life parody

Homeric convention. Achilles' dilemma, a conflict of individual and social obligation, is modulated to the issue of freedom in a social process that insists on conformity. Yet Bond appropriates only the violent and rapacious instinct of the Homeric hero. Since indiviual self-assertion is prized in the *Iliad*, Bond fashions his male protagonist as an elitist militarist whose "assertion" implies a totalitarianism that justifies itself in order to secure power. The glory of personal triumph and the competitive energy that infuses the Homeric poem is renegotiated by Heros into easy butchery, fantasies of a "New Athens," and world domination. If Homer reasserts the elemental bonds of kinship at the end of the epic, Bond's Heros endorses a process of dehumanization until it becomes evident that he must be stopped.

The Homeric justification of conquest idealized the concept of worth through personal style and prowess. Bond ironically plays off the Greek word "heros" to confer an ironic distinction on the preeminent spokesman of Athenian authority in the play. Individuating Heros as a "hero" provides the most immediate context through which Bond deconstructs the remote and terrifying stature of an Ajax or Achilles. Such figures, C.M. Bowra comments,

> ...faced their problems bravely and squarely and said exactly what they meant about them. There is not irony, deceit, no concealment. This brave candor reflects the self-regard which inspires heroic behavior.[10]

Homer's Greece, however, is a community antithetical to Heros' world as well as to our own. Rather than the fulfillment of libidinous psychic drives, the code implies the elevation of the self to a transcendent status. Yet the world of *The Woman* is scaled to a particularly non-heroic human size; man is no longer judged by any absolute measure but only against the pale image of his own conduct. The justice he obtains, Bond insists, is no longer the measure of Zeus' Golden Scales, but the result of his own legislation. In *The Woman*, the urge to divinity has been replaced by Bond's more modest aspirations for humanity. Throughout *The Woman*, he reveals an implicit critique of the myth of the individual--the idea of absolute selfhood that has shaped the consciousness and created the dislocation of life in the twentieth century. Heros' policy of Pax Athenea and his creation of a thriving New Athens is conceived through a policy of colonization and enslavement. It is a policy that formalizes a will to power in order to gratify its own messianic impulses.

Despite the lethalness of its subject, the *Iliad's* assessment of war as a mythic conflict and apotheosis of human achievement has been ratified by events in the twentieth century. Bond opposes the idea of war as a socially validated way of life; his example of the destruction of community and the self-assertion in *The Woman* amounts to a political and social revision of Homer's poem, rather than an aesthetic disclaimer to Homer's art. The mutual suspicion of the Greeks and Trojans resembles East/West tensions and reflects the political turbulence of the cold war in the fifties and sixties. The figure of Heros especially defines the demagogic leaders of the twentieth century.

Simone Weil, whose long essay, *The Iliad as a Poem of Force*, written in 1943 in occupied France, supplies an analysis of the poem that furnishes a theoretical justification for the play, much the way Peter Brook made use of Jan Kott's celebrated essay on *Endgame*. I don't think Bond necessarily read Weil's monograph, but *The Woman* dramatizes Weil's argument that the poem's subject is brute, compulsive force:

> Force employed by man, force that enslaves man, force before which man's flesh shrinks away. In this work...the human spirit is shown as modified by its relations with force, as swept away, blinded, by the very force it imagined it could handle, as deformed by the weight of the force it submits to. For those dreamers who considered that force, thanks to progress, would soon be a thing of the past, the *Iliad* could appear as an historical document.[11]

Like Bond, Weil perceived force as the perverse center of human action and substitutes her own spiritual categories for Homer's. Even a world of elevated style cannot disguise the horrific events and indiscriminate suffering instigated by the capitulation to force.

For Heros, death is an abstraction meted out in various quantities, theatrical gestures in which lives are destroyed like toys, acts accomplished in response to a vague, self-defined political necessity: restless soldiers, Pax Athenea, the deployment of political strategies or the need to solidify a political base. Bond rejects the necessity of grief and annihilation that clings to "heroes," and suggests a mode of apprehending reality that rests within the scope of our own age: the exploration of the tension between oppressor (Heros, the Son, men) and oppressed (Ismene, Hecuba, women). In the *Iliad*, female, slave, suppliant and conquerer coexist in a familiar, if conventional hierarchy. The defeated lament in a stylized prosody and express their anguish according to poetic convention. A proper formula expresses mourning for a king or a son, just as victory is hailed in particular epithets. Such constructs insulate us from grief and presume an aristocratic, almost feudal power structure which restricts feeling according to social position. If for Homer, death is meted out with geometric rigor and man is fated to suffer, albeit valorously, *The Woman* transforms the relation of destiny to selfhood, and democratizes Homeric fate. Heros, the aristocratic general of the military industrial complex is struck down by the archetypal representative of the proletariat; boundaries are drawn between worker-slave and capitalist-militarist. If *The Woman* and the *Iliad* are two different studies of the psychology of power and the subjugation of the human spirit to force, Bond focuses on the social results of such pressure, Homer on the valor that accrues to such prowess. For each, something remains futile about the pursuit of power. No one is capable of holding or possessing force for long.

If Homer provides a philosophic departure for *The Woman*, Euripides originates an image of human suffering and annihilation that has captivated the classical imagination from Erasmus, to Dante, to the "mobled Queen" of *Hamlet*. The image of *The Woman* is a composite of two women in Bond's play--Hecuba, the central figure in Euripides' *The Trojan Woman* and *Hecuba*, and a figure of Bond's own imagination, Ismene. The wife of Heros provides a contrast to her husband's ruthlessness and furnishes the spirit of dissent that enables Hecuba to formulate the plan for the death of the Greek General. A nominal ambassador through which Heros hopes to convince Hecuba of his own good faith, Ismene's growth is measured by the recognition of her delegation's insincerity. Gradually conscious of the policy and spirit of the Greek necessity which demands the destruction of the city, she allies herself with Hecuba and remains in Troy as a hostage until the Greeks depart. While her dissent is ensured, her personal safety is not; she is immured in a wall surrounding the city and left to hear the dying wails of the massacred. Restored to freedom when pillaging Greeks steal her jewels, then gathered aboard a Greek slave ship with Hecuba and the statue, the two find a haven on a remote island when a storm destroys their vessel; the statue is lost in the sea.

By the second half of the play, Ismene's experience has left her partially disabled and only half-conscious of events. She and Hecuba, who has blinded one eye at the sight of her city's destruction, have evolved as mother and daughter. Yet after years of relative peace, the Greeks return; Heros remains obsessed by a need to possess the statue, if only to ensure his political ascendency.

If *The Woman* is a composite of three images of femaleness, the statue also presides over the second half of the play. The icon which polarizes male and female values is an abstraction that possesses no intrinsic value to

Hecuba and Ismene and bears little spiritual connection to the men. A parody of sexual possession, its ownership implies masculine bravado and the accumulation of potency that ironically implies a rejection of feminine virtues. The goddess is a negative image that brings plague, death and starvation. And it cannot avoid the stigma of being female--the Trojan rabble chant "bitch, bitch, bitch," as it is carried out of the city and surrendered to the Greeks. Yet it provides Bond with a resonant dramatic symbol that focuses the male aspirations in the play: Heros' destructive energies, the internal factionalism of each camp, and the rivalry of the Greek and Trojan priests. At the same time, it projects the ambiguity of possession and female sexuality.

Entrapped in a loveless marriage to an old man whose purpose was to rejuvenate himself, Hecuba retains little faith in the efficacy of passion; but the idea of female dissent is not tolerated in the masculine world of the Greeks or Trojans. Yet it devolves upon Hecuba to act, not so much as a woman but as any moral figure who insists that history must not repeat itself. By trusting her own instincts and subverting diplomacy into a ruthless form of her own necessity, she appropriates male prerogatives in order to overthrow them. By the end of the play, she alone possesses the ability to act efficiently, to conceptualize a plan, and disingenuously promote its success. Like Lear, she undergoes a process of "enforced education," of loss, exhaustion and withdrawal. While Lear's education is partially imaged in the process Ismene undergoes in Part I, it is Hecuba who emerges as the figure who ensures the future by acting in the present.

In Euripides' *Hecuba*, the Trojan Queen is left devasted--"too old, too weak to stand." She bitterly laments the sacrifice of her daughter at Achilles' tomb and the treacherous murder of her son by an ally. Bond recalibrates Hecuba's lamentation in *The Woman* and perhaps found the impulse for his own play in Odysseus' mocking words to the prostrate Queen: "Remember your weakness and accept this tragic loss as best you can. Nothing you can do or say can change the facts. Under the circumstances the logical course is resignation."[12] Bond's Queen transcends her loss and is empowered by the playwright to reject the masculine accusation of female hysteria formalized by Heros' suggestion that she hang herself. Heros, like Odysseus, resorts to manipulation through gender roles--deliberate obfuscation, ironic courtesy, and elliptical argument that deprive Hecuba and Ismene of their selfhood. Bond repudiates Euripides' conservatism, particularly the arguments of the chorus that human nature never seems to change; evil remains evil. He denies his protagonist any respite from the pressures of the world, whether it's the leisure of solitude or the luxury of her own grief. Isolated for twelve years and partially blind, she is hardly an image of potency. But she endures, rallies, and rejects Heros' attempts to destroy her life a second time. When Euripides' figure learns of the murder of her son, she is activated by vengeance and like Bond's heroine, plots the downfall of a man. But she is implicated by the barbarity of her revenge. Euripides modulates his heroine's pain from pathos and dependence to a gesture daemonic in its exaction. The murder of Polymestor's children is a passionate response rather than an act of political necessity devised with planning and calculation. In *The Woman*, Hecuba's actions are enacted not in the spirit of vengeance but by a moral impulse to ensure the continuity of life. The chorus' implication that no man is free, all are slaves of money and necessity, dramatizes the compulsion of the male figures in each play. Like Odysseus, Heros is a demagogue, decisive in action, alive to the idea of compassion but not allowing it to affect his consideration.

Rather than embodying a rhythm of suffering followed by savage revenge, *The Trojan Women* elaborates the illogic of political necessity and the difference between those who hold power and those who suffer under it. As we watch Hecuba engaged in successive stages of grief, she is stripped of all value and integrity. She remains the victim of a brutal, insensate necessity devised by men who are corrupted by a power they barely comprehend. Like Heros, Odysseus claims that necessity leaves him no choice, yet he is revealed by the tangled web of his own logic.

If Odysseus conforms to the spokesman for male authority in *Hecuba*, Talthybius urges silence and passivity, the emblematic truth for female captives in *The Trojan Women*:

> "Do not fight it. Take your grief as you were meant to take it, give up the struggle....You are in our power. How can women hope to struggle against the arms of Greeks?"[13]

In the play, Hecuba's energy is misdirected; unable to comprehend the nature of her genuine oppressors, she directs her enmity against Helen, the most immediate and tangible cause of her grief and the figure who remains within the scope of her vengeance. Despite her arguments, Menelaus is beguiled by Helen's beauty; the play ends as Hecuba is led inconsolably away. The victim of accruing disasters, her acceptance implies a rhythm of unfulfilled hope followed by accelerating despair. She finds herself in the ritualized role of victim, acted upon and forced to yield to misfortune.

In both of Euripides' plays women function to support and maintain male institutions. Procreation, the ability to bear male heirs, remains their only claim on history and events. Even Cassandra's gift of prophecy in *The Trojan Women* is ironically mocked--she is condemned to be misunderstood. Bond, however, frees Ismene and Hecuba from the causality of gender biased roles. *The Woman* rejects a tradition of idealism that implies that Euripides' play glimpses a scale of values in which, Gilbert Murray suggests,

> There is something--call it glory, or splendor or, for lack of a better name, beauty--something at any rate which is material for eternal song, in playing one's part to the last world and enduring what fate sends.[14]

The idea of splendor in affliction, sublimity in slavery, and exhaustion in despair, reflects an appeal to emotion and grief that annuls the possibility of constructive change. In *The Woman*, Bond refuses to use Hecuba as a symbol of sorrow whose lamentations echo in front of an empty temple. Bond refuses to ratify the idea of unrelieved despair, especially when it radiates from a male-empowered hierarchy. He refuses to defer female prerogatives to the process of history. Instead, he creates characters who are unable to express their autonomy; like men, they participate in the creation of history and are essential to the production of a rational society. In *The Woman*, Bond transforms figures paralyzed by bereavement and the loss of moral identity into figures of energy and consciousness. He refuses to allow the old tragic pathos to mediate their lives, and permit their self-absorption as passive victims of male potency.

At the same time, *The Woman* implies a critique of the male power structure. Bond's Trojan War is precipitated by the theft by Priam of the Goddess of Good Fortune. At the beginning of the play, the female icon has failed to rejuvenate Priam; he succumbs to age. Heros' obsessiveness prolongs the myth of the statue and its significance. Though we never meet Priam, we might assume that Heros stands in as his surrogate. The sinuosity of his logic links the statue's possession to his own grandiose designs:

> The statue brings good fortune only to those destined to own her. But how can we win the war and capture the Goddess of Good Fortune when we haven't got the statue to give us the good fortune to win the war? (p. 5)

Like all "visionary" imaginations, Heros presumes that the statue empowers him to repossess her; he simply responds "to the call of the divinity." Trojan impiety, he insists, is to "hold...the supreme goddess against her will" (p. 15). Heros' policy belies any gesture of compromise, and implicates him in the necessity of Troy's destruction, if only to preserve and enhance his own political base. His motives are revealed to Ismene when he recalls the game of sacking Troy he played as a child and announces, "It's a closed coffin with someone moving inside" (p. 20). In order to deflect her arguments, he archly contends how difficult it is to control troops in the last days of a war. Musing on his own messianic aspiration, he declares, "I'm a god to my men..." (p. 20), and finally claims, "The voice is clear to me." A seasoned politician, he artfully defuses Ismene's pleas with elliptical arguments, and implies Troy will be spared if she relinquishes the statue: "If I make mistakes I'm punished--by the government, or the troops, or God" (p. 20). Yet his final rationale to Ismene is a paradox, a terrifying image of brute compulsion designed to pay tribute to his leadership:

> If I left Troy tomorrow, Troy would attack us--or someone else would attack Troy. When will there be peace? When we honor virtue...the New Athens will stand for that...when people suffer they'll remember Athens. It will be the last thing many people will see before they go mad" (p. 54).

As he exhorts his troops to victory, the soldiers hail the Goddess, sharpen their axes, and pray for the guidance of their blades. Heros' attitude towards women is concretized after he has sentenced Ismene to death. Along with the Son's accusation that Hecuba is capable of seducing the gods, it is another instance of sexual politics in the play:

> I've made love to you but you're still a virgin. If...the army raped you on the corner of Troy tomorrow, you'd still be a virgin. You receive nothing, only give. All women are virgins when they're faced with murder. (p. 54)

The politics of patriarchy reemerge when Hecuba appropriates a masculine mode of action (the act of self-blinding) and is consequently degraded by Greek soldiers who chant, "Bitch, bitch, bitch." In response to her appeal that Astynax be spared, Heros vows, "He'll die and you'll see his body" (p. 59). In her grief he counsels her to respond as her femaleness demands: "Find a beam and hang youself" (p. 60). In a last attempt to oppose Heros, Hecuba relies on a typically feminine gestures of conciliation, an effort to win favor through submission. "Teach me," she beseeches,

> Not how to herd women through the streets and goad them with your swords so you can chase them, or how to jeer when the old run and fall down, or how to mock when you lean over them with your sword, or kill a woman and wipe the knife in her husband's gray beard, or throw a man's blood down on his own doorstep--not all these skills of violence... (p. 57)

In a rejection of the world's causality, Hecuba decides never again to gaze upon human destructiveness and blinds herself in one eye. Like Oedipus, the process invests her with a new sanctity and authority in the second half of the play.

After twelve years of relative peace in a primitive island culture, Hecuba and Ismene cling self-protectively to one another. But their condition remains fundamentally unchanged. Bond observes:

> I'm certainly not saying that the community is idyllic. I'm saying that it will have to face the problem of the Greeks. It will eventually be invaded and colonized.[15]

The Greeks arrive at Heros' behest, still seeking to recover the statue. Their initial words suggest the same duplicity: "Don't be alarmed," cries Nestor, "I'm your friend" (p. 69), he proclaims as he offers Hecuba "sanctuary" and describes his "New World" of painted palaces, blooming laurels and fountains. Through Pax Athenea, "The world is reconciled" (p. 70). Yet his words belie his weariness. Athens is decaying--"breaking down"--property and lives need protecting. And the world is clearly not reconciled as long as Heros possesses the ability to recreate his destruction of Troy. Yet the predominate impulse of the second half of the play is not so much the intrusion of the Greeks, but Hecuba's realization that withdrawal is impossible. Though she insists, "I don't want to remember," force must be met and neutralized. An opportunity arises when an escaped slave from the Athenian silver mines arrives on the island and seeks sanctuary. She tells the man:

> He must be killed! I've walked on the beach and daydreamed of killing him myself, sheer fantasy! I'm blind and I haven't enough strength to scratch him with a pin. He'd chop you down like a stick. (p. 90)

Heros' pursuit of the psychic wholeness that the statue embodies finally does lead him to the island. Hecuba recognizes the proud rhetoric, the hollow bravado, and the obsessive hunger to possess. Yet her impulse is to withdraw and be left alone. She admits to Ismene, "I left the world when my children were killed" (p. 81), yet, as the Greeks came closer to repeating the events of Troy, she overcomes the idea that the "dead are dead" and "the past is past." The memory of Troy infuses the present; if we don't learn from the past, it will continue to haunt us, Bond tells us. When Hecuba cries, "I can't change the whole world" (p. 77), the logic of events refutes her, but Hero's self-destructive obsession with the icon subjects him to Hecuba's authority:

> You're strong. You have nothing and want nothing, so you have nothing to lose. Yet you have what I want. No power on earth can move you, I'm in your power. I've never been in this situation before. (p. 81)

Hecuba's blindness and age invest her with a numinous quality that ordains a show of deference: "I killed your family, destroyed your home. Of course I was raving with war madness" (p. 87). Heros reveals his philosophy of power divested of all pretense, as if Hecuba could neither comprehend nor react to his political principles: "A leader really needs only one virtue, restraint---but many vices. A good ruler knows how to hate....How else can he make the people afraid?" (p. 89). The idea of wanton bloodshed and the image of Troy smouldering in ruins is blithely recapitulated. If the statue is not recovered, Heros implies, he must provide evidence of his efforts--"the painful destruction of these islands and the razing of the village. I have a duty to Athens not to let chance make me a laughing stock. I take a duty to Athens very seriously (p. 90).

Yet Hecuba artfully manipulates Heros' fixation with a ruse that integrates the idea of religious prophecy with his vanity, sense of competition, and the occasion of the village festival. She recalls a "dream" in which a race decided the beneficiary of the newly recovered statue; the loser is executed. Hecuba's revelation of the crippled Man as Heros' opponent reveals a class antagonism that is exacerbated by the Man's inability to acknowledge his name--he is simply a product of the mines:

MAN. When you built your new city our hell grew
with it. It's not true the guilty go to
hell; only the weak.

HEROS. Enemies of the state are criminals!

MAN. I was born there....I took your statue in
Athens. You think I'm the broken bits that
were chipped away! No--I made their smile.

HEROS. I didn't make the world.

MAN. Only Athens.

HEROS. Things change. Step by step. Let them out
they'd starve.

MAN. You don't want them to dirty your new street.

HEROS. (offers his hand) If I win this race...then
I'll do what I can to help those people.

MAN. (refusing his hand) You'll go away and forget. Every second of my life--till I ran--was
watched by people like you--holding a whip
with a silver handle. (pp. 97-98)

Hecuba advises the man to wait patiently in his hut; Heros arrives, breathless and apparently victorious: "...for once--I cannot lose. The truth speaks for me, Hecuba! I don't administer justice now. It shouts my name" (p. 104). It is the ironic truth of victory, but not of the play and not of justice. Hecuba reveals she has witnessed a different race in which Heros sat mesmerized by a tree, while the Man emerged as the winner. Hecuba speaks portentously of how the image of the Goddess has possessed Heros' rationality:. "You smiled. You didn't blink. The Goddess had trapped you under a tree....You knew nothing of what had happened to you" (p. 105). The nature of Heros' obsession is reframed almost surreptitiously, and though it is unclear whether he comprehends Hecuba's words, Heros is struck down by the Man with a sword Hecuba supplies. Bond's dramatic logic insists that Heros' irrationality

> should appear to lead inevitably to his death, because through this Bond seeks to illustrate the idea that an irrational society carries within it the seeds of its own destruction. The Dark Man is identified as the representative of a new working-class consciousness. It is he who kills Heros, because the death must seem the result of historical, rather than tragic, inevitability.[16]

What must be equally clear is that Hecuba's motivation is not simply vengeance but a revolutionary act: "I show them," Bond comments, "acting out the logical development of history. And...I have represented history as a woman with a sword under her skirt."[17] By seizing control of events, Hecuba incarnates Bond's image of human purpose acting rationally within an historical framework in order to oppose a "diseased culture."

When Nestor calls for vengeance, Hecuba's words--"Remember Troy, the cost," (p. 106)--are heeded for the first time on their own terms, rather than as a woman's lament. The Greeks depart peacefully, but Hecuba, like Oedipus and Lear, is not permitted to witness the growth of a new culture. She is destroyed by a storm, a symbolic correlative of her own act of purification. Yet Bond leaves the audience with no facile solutions: "In a way the community at the end is like the young people at the end of *Lear*. The problem of the future has to be faced."[18] Though there are few guarantees, Ismene and the Man possess a new, self-created independence. If *The Woman* acknowledges the difficulty and hardship implicit in surviving in the world, it remains a world in which, Bond insists, "Freedom is possible."[19]

ENDNOTES

[1] Joseph F. McCrindle, ed., *Behind the Scenes* (New York: Holt Rinehart and Winston, 1971), pp. 135-136.

[2] Edward Bond, "Scenes of War and Freedom: A Short Essay," in *The Woman* (London: Eyre Methuen, 1979), p. 136.

[3] Malcolm Hay and Philip Roberts, "Edward Bond: Stages in a Life," *Observor Magazine* (August 6, 1978), p. 13.

[4] Ibid., p. 13.

[5] Hay and Roberts, p. 251.

[6] Charles Fourier, "Théories Des Quartres Movements," in *Oeuvres Completes* (1841) I, p. 195; cited in Juliet Mitchell, *Woman's Estate* (New York: Vintage Books, 1973), p. 77.

[7] Op. cit., No. 5, pp. 249-250.

[8] Harold Hobson, "*The Woman*: Plays in Performance," *Drama* (Autumn, 1978), p. 43.

[9] Op. cit., No. 5, p. 43.

[10] C.M. Bowra, *Tradition and Design in the Iliad*, (Westport, CT: Greenwood Press, 1977), p. 113.

[11] Simone Weil, *The Iliad as a Poem of Force* (Wallingford, PA: Pendle Hill, 1968), p. 3.

[12] William Arrowsmith and Richard Lattimore, eds., *Hecuba*, trans. Wm. Arrowsmith, *Euripides III* (Chicago: University of Chicago Press, 1958), p. 18.

[13] William Arrowsmith and Richmond Lattimore, eds., *The Trojan Women*, trans. Richmond Lattimore, *Euripides III*, p. 154.

[14] Gilbert Murray, *Euripides and His Age* (London: Oxford University Press, 1965), p. 219.

[15] Op. cit., No. 5. p. 256.

[16] Ibid., p. 261.

[17] Ibid., p. 239.

[18] Ibid., p. 262.

[19] Op. cit., No. 2, p. 136.

Chapter 9

CONCLUSION

This history of British drama since 1956 is a history of a loss of faith: an account of the dissolution of radical dreams and a socialist welfare state in post-war Britain. The English stage has become more and more a place for political and social analysis--a means to scrutinize the failure of the hopeful optimism that informed the post-war period. David Edgar explains in his essay, "Ten Years of Political Theatre," that the socialist theatre's increased concerns with militancy in the early seventies began with a rejection of writers like Arnold Wesker and John Osborne in favor of a form that "demonstrates the social and political character of human behavior."[1] It is a theatre that "does not begin with the individual but with the problem."[2]

In this framework, the work of Edward Bond has progressively reflected a conflict between liberal humanism and revolutionary socialism that has gained ascendency among two generations of English dramatists that include John Arden and Margaret D'Arcy, Trevor Griffiths as well as younger figures like David Hare, Howard Brenton, David Edgar, and Howard Barker. If these playwrights do not precisely regard the future of society as "a self-conscious collective" (as Bond does), they all have come to equate moral self-consciousness with socialist self-consciousness. They all ascribe to Piscator's belief about the function of political theatre:

> The business of revolutionary theatre is to take reality as its point of departure and to magnify the social discrepency, making it an element of our indictment, our revolt, our new order.[3]

Theatre provides a medium to discuss public life, a platform to assess the past, evaluate the present, and hyposthesize about the future. It is necessarily a locus of disillusion and militancy. Rather than assess blame, it refutes the disavowal of responsibility created by failed political and social institutions. In the best of all possible worlds, it is a place of judgement--the "best court"[4] society can have. Rather than a supplier of relief or of spurious entertainment, it comprises the "last public place for a critical but humane judgement of a monstrous speculative society."[5] Its commitment to alter society's social and political base defy solipsism and invoke a Brechtian necessity that not only insists on interpreting the world but on changing it. At the same time, the need to create a new perception of society and a "new" socialist theatre differs from Brecht's Epic stage

> ...not because of an egotistical wish to be different but because the world has given us more to account for and the leap in scientific knowledge allows us to look even closer at the nature of man.

Bond adds, "We should begin with Brecht, but we shouldn't end there."[6]

Yet Bond's assessment reflects an optimism in the potential of theatre that is unverified by empirical evidence. Whether articulated in the Oxonian accents of Hare and Barker, the manifestos of Arden and D'Arcy, the polemics of John McGrath, the articles of David Edgar, or the prefaces of Edward Bond, the British political theatre establishment has created a vast, articulate rationale for its existence. Its exhortations are conceived in an energetic belief in the creation of a new theatre and a new society. Yet so far, no unification or consensus of spirit has mobilized any segment of British society. No newly emerged working-class consciousness has succeeded in polarizing public opinion. In fact, the ideologues of the movment have begun to resign themselves to recalibrating the measure of their accomplishment. David Edgar, in a recent article acknowledges that theatre "can't change the world overnight or send its audiences out to build barricades."⁷ John McGrath admits that, "Theatre can never cause a social change."⁸ And Bond concludes that theatre "can't by itself change the world."⁹ Yet they all seem to recognize the capacity of theatre to articulate a collective voice and formulate solidarity through a common determination. Though it is not clear precisely how, they all agree with Bond that theatre can aid those who are involved in changing society and evolving a new consciousness.

In any enduring culture, the artist is the recipient of a set of assumptions about empirical reality--the relation between people and their connection with the environment. The act of creation implies the necessity of recovering a form out of the quality of experience that reflects the artist's sensibility. However, in times of extreme cultural stress and human crisis, values don't match experience; the shape of reality becomes more problematic. The impulse of the artist in the first half of the twentieth century has been to seek a coherent pattern of experience through subjective memory, emotion and internalized thought. The most empirical ground for such a prognosis and self-inventory is autobiographical; it implies the failure of social and political experience to bestow value. In *Sons and Lovers*, *Portrait of the Artist*, and *Remembrance of Things Past*, the ego only minimally retains its social preeminence and essentially retires into the recesses of the self. The fiction and drama of Beckett as well as the work of Pinter, Handke, Genet, and Robert Wilson explore the residual mystery of the self through a metaphysics of ambiguity and uncertainty that employs solipsism, the inability to communicate, and the failure of language to suggest a dysfunctionalism at the basis of human activity. Antithetically, Edward Bond and two generations of English playwrights insist on art that is congruent with life; art that does not simply concern itself with men but the order of things--a historical compulsion that places individuals at cross purposes with their ability to function in their environment. Bond's condition of urgency enacts a theatre of commitment whose political import provides a more ambitious objective than creating an enduring work of art--devising a rational society. Bond rejects the impulse to reorder the materials of his own experience through aesthetic form in order to possess an imaginative grasp of the world. Instead, he creates artist figures, imaginative recreations of his own persona who have the capacity to act, choose, and bear responsibility for their actions. Piscator questioned how theatre can

> take the liberty of ignoring the lives of those people down there while it indulges in a display of intellectual abstractions, formal arabesques, challengings from its own imagination. It must be real, real to the last detail, unreservedly true, if it wants to capture even a reflection of those people's lives.[10]

Bond's poet protagonists enact a form of the playwright's own destiny by combating institutionalized and "legitimated tyranny." In their struggle, they become symbols of culture, destined not only to be a part of history, but its active representatives. They combine character, class function and historical situation in an image that transforms the world of appearances into human connections. Like Bond, they refuse to exalt an inhuman reality and search for a form to express their refusal. If art expresses a vision of the world at a precise time and place, the artist must subsist within the range and possibilities offered by his society; he cannot be indifferent to the relations in whose framework he creates. Readers who expect a theatre of traditionally memorable characters or who anticipate a widening circle of unfolding complexities will be disappointed. Bond's provocativeness does not lay in partial revelations, in disclosing the scope of evil or uncovering the transcendence of man entrapped in a tangled web not clearly of his own creation. He is didactic; a conscious moralist whose concerns provide a means for us to live so that our moral freedom is not jeopardized. Perhaps these are not profound assertions. Is it perhaps an oversimplification to argue that

> ...people are naturally good....What they are depends on society...in a good society it is natural for them to be kind. If they are evil, that too has to be created.[11]

For readers accustomed to dealing with the deconstruction of a text, the assurance and the apparent ease with which "answer plays" are summarily served up provide a degree of uncertainty:

> We mustn't write only problem plays, we must write answer plays--or at least plays which make answers clearer and more practical. When I wrote my first plays, I was, naturally, conscious of the weight of the problems. Now I've become more conscious of the strength of human beings to provide answers. The answers aren't always light, easy or even straightforward but the purpose--a socialist society---is clear.[12]

Does Bond's exploration of reality represent experience as unproblematic and susceptible to rational analysis? Does he confront artistic problems with dramatically facile and insufficient resolutions? These questions originate with the form of ideological drama and the rationale provided for its existence. C.L. Bigsby argues that ideological drama is "the expression of the need to close aesthetic and social spaces" in order for the disjunction between "appearance and essence to coincide."[13] Ambiguity implies an irrationality that suggests experience is "not wholly subverted to rational analysis."[14] The prefaces, prologues, countless interviews and even the self-demystifying responses to inquiries reiterate, overlap, and crystalize the Marxist humanism of *The Economic and Philosophic Manuscripts*. While they provide clarity in a world where ambiguity is sought and often assumed, the sheer weight of words perhaps does the playwright a disservice not unlike his self-prescribed "Rational Theatre." The self-defined notion of a "Rational Theatre," and the idea of explanatory prefaces suggests an uncertainty of the plays alone to sustain the kind of response and analysis the author requires.

Yet Bond's imagination transcends a merely "Rational Theatre." The plays possess more mystery, invention and poetry than the prefaces imply. At the same time, Bond's symbolic imagination surmounts the dissent of critics who accuse the playwright of "...the cliché of nature of [his]...positive program, which comes expressed in an easiness of achievement that is dramatically unjustified."[15] The argument that Bond creates expressly false cultures that issue in polemically oppressive figures is an oversimplification itself, and overlooks the purpose of Bond's fables. His intention is not mystification. In a recent interview he claims his later plays are about "rhapsody...which is in praise of human beings."[16] Bond makes it unconditionally clear that in them "right triumphs over bad." In *The Woman*, the waste of war is contasted to a symbolic celebration of "human tenacity and insight."[17]

Bond's plays locate the individual at a juncture in history in which an isolated figure must decide whether he can afford to be a hero. Each figure possesses a vitality, individuated and activated by political and economic facts yet localized by the objective framework of his social existence. Bond's artists remain men of partial imagination who fail in the quest for psychic wholeness. If destiny, as George Lukcás contends, comes to the hero from without, "the vital centre of character and intersecting point of man and his destiny do not necessarily coincide..."[18] Though Lukács' analysis of the heroes of the "new drama" as passive rather than active figures may seem prescriptive, it partly accounts for the duality of passion and complacency in Bond's figures:

> ...they are acted upon more than they act for themselves; they defend rather than attack; their heroism is mostly a heroism of anguish, of despair, not one of bold aggressiveness. Since so much of the inner man has fallen prey to destiny, the last battle is to be enacted within.[19]

Yet individual success is less important than the scope and urgency of the issues that affect them. Clare, Shakespeare, Basho, and Lear have little effect on their own communities. However, they are not hopelessly or inevitably fated; each is wrenched out of his complacency and is forced to recognize issues that confront him. Each lives a passionate, felt existence in which a network of circumstances transcends his own particular destiny.

If Bond's major theme is the violence which "shapes and obsesses our society,"[20] his plays seek to explore the causes and effects of such behavior. They provide the rationale for the stoning of the baby in *Saved*, the gouging out of Lear's eyes, and the disfigurement of Tiger in *The Bundle*. Violence provides a technique of disruption that David Edgar tells us has been incorporated into recent English drama to confront "...the gap between the objective crisis of the system and the subjective responses of human being within it."[21] Bond's dissent transmits the nature of that crisis with unparalleled urgency:

> All our culture, education, industrial and legal organization is directed to the task of killing (people psychologically and emotionally). That is why such law and order societies bear the responsibility for the oppression they create.[22]

By any standards, Bond's theatre is not for aesthetes any more than it is an article for consumption by audiences who wish to escape self-knowledge. His theatrical images mediate the historical momentousness of an action as well as its dramatic impetus: the gibbeted woman in *Bingo*, Lear shovelling earth in the shadow of the wall, Clare discussing literature with Admiral Radstock as two boxers pummel themselves as a backdrop, are each devised as instances that reconcile pure dramatic action and subjective analysis. And in the twenty-five years that he has been writing, the message remains essentially unchanged. The aesthetic: to "use the theatre as a way of testing reality--if a thing can't be made to be accepted by an audience as plausible and practical on stage...it can't be plausible...in life,"[23] persists. If

"Marxism," Terry Eagleton comments in his Preface to *Marxism and Literary Criticism*, "is a scientific theory of human society and of the practice of transforming them,"[24] Bond's theatre devises an imaginative enactment of the transforming process. It is the primacy of history in Bond's plays that tests his assumptions--from the corrupt power politics of the Trojan War, to the aggressive capitalism of *The Bundle*, to the feudal order that legitimates violence in *The Fool* and *Bingo*. In dramatizing the dialectic of history and society, the function of art remains to "interpret the world and not merely mirror it."[25] Interpretation implies a criticism of the irrational base of society, the result of its class structure. By placing the individual in history, Bond hopes to unfix the old view of a system that appears unalterable. Though his artist figures never triumph, we as audience members witness, though the characters may not, the larger focus of history. Yet Bond never diminishes the extraordinary sense of anguish his characters undergo. Lukács' formulation of the dynamic between external pressure and personal fate helps to clarify the shape of Bond's dramaturgy:

> ...the more the vital motivating center is displaced outward (i.e., the greater the determining force of external factors), the more the center of tragic conflict is drawn inward; it becomes internalized, more exclusively a conflict in the spirit.[26]

As we share the learning process of the character's lives, we glimpse the possiblity of a new totality, models of behavior in which to act or refrain from action, to be heroic or not has grave consequences. The plays question what happens to consciousness caught between individual and social morality, what happens to men entrapped by the ruling group that maintains them. Through their failings--Heros' madness, Basho's indifference, and Shakespeare's inability to act, Bond's characters exhort us to recover a sense of destiny in our lives, to implement change in an order which places individuals at odds with the structure of society. Thus, it is an essential element of

Bond's dramaturgy that the lives of his protagonists are unconditionally formulated, explicted and analyzed. Despite the inability of Clare, Shakespeare, or Lear to make peace with themselves, Bond's almost romantic faith in the possibility of change sustains in his audience a faith in human endurance; progress may be problemmatic, but as Raymond Williams tells us, "To take a meaning from experience, and try to make it active, is in fact our process of growth."[27]

ENDNOTES

[1] Edward Bond, "On Brecht: A Letter to Peter Holland," p. 33.

[2] Walter Sokel, "Brecht's Split Characters and His Sense of the Tragic," *Brecht: A Collection of Critical Essays* (Englewood: Prentice Hall, 1962), p. 134.

[3] Erwin Piscator, *The Political Theatre: A History*, trans. Hugh Rorrison (New York: 197), p. 188.

[4] David Hare, "From Portable Theatre to Joint Stock...via Shaftesbury Avenue," *Theatre Quarterly* 5, No. 20 (1975-76), p. 114.

[5] Howard Barker in *Contemporary Dramatists*, ed., James Vinson, second edition (London: St. James Press, 1977), p. 34.

[6] Op. cit., No. 1, p. 34.

[7] David Edgar, "Theatre, Politics and the Working Class," *London Tribune*, 22 April 1977.

[8] John McGrath, "The Year of the Cheviot," *Plays and Players*, February 1974, p. 30.

[9] Edward Bond, "A Note on Dramatic Method," *The Bundle*, p. xiii.

[10] Op. cit., No. 3 p. 329.

[11] *Companion*, p. 26.

[12] Ibid., p. 75.

[13] Bigsby, p. 23.

[14] Ibid., p. 23.

[15] Christopher Innes, "The Political Spectrum of Bond," in *Modern British Dramatists*, ed., J.R. Brown (Englewood Cliffs: Prentice Hall, 1984), p. 146.

[16] Christopher Innes, "Edward Bond: From Rationalism to Rhapsody," *Canadian Theatre Review*, No. 23 (Summer 1979), p. 108.

[17] Ibid., p. 108.

[18] Lukács, p. 436.

[19] Ibid., p. 429.

[20] Edward Bond, "Author's Preface" to *Lear*, *Plays: Two*, p. 3.

[21] David Edgar, "Ten Years of Political Theatre, 1968-1978," *Theatre Quarterly*, 8, No. 32. (1979), pp. 31-32.

[22] Op. cit., No. 15, p. 130.

[23] Op. cit., No. 11, p. 74.

[24] Terry Eagleton, *Marxism and Literary Criticism* (London: Eyre Methuen, 1976), p. 17.

[25] Op. cit., No 11, p. 74.

[26] Op. cit., No. 18, p. 429.

[27] *Culture and Society*, p. 338.

BIBLIOGRAPHY

Ansorge, Peter. *Disrupting the Spectacle: Five Years of Experimental and Fringe Theatre in Britain*, London: Pitman House, 1975.

_____. "Directors in Interview, No. 2; Jane Howell." *Plays and Players*, October 1968, 70.

Arnold, Arthur. "Lines of Development in Bond's Plays." *Theatre Quarterly*, 2, No. 5 (1972), 15-19.

Barker, Howard. "Playwrights, Politics, and Catherine Itzin." *London Tribune*, 23 September 1977

Berger, John. *Art and Revolution*. London: Penguin, 1969.

Barth, Adolph K.H. "The Aggressive 'Theatrum Mundi' of Edward Bond: *Narrow Road to the Deep North*." *Modern Drama*, 18 (1975), 189-200.

Bigsby, C.W.E., editor. *Contemporary English Drama*. New York: Holmes and Meier, 1981.

_____. "The Language of Crises in British Theatre: The Drama of Cultural Pathology," in *Contemporary English Drama*, 19-52.

Bock, Hedwig and Wertheim, Albert, editors. *Essays on Contemporary British Dramatists*. Munich: Hueber, 1981.

Bond, Edward. *Edward Bond Plays: One*. London: Eyre Methuen, 1977.

_____. *Edward Bond Plays: Two*. London: Eyre Methuen, 1978.

_____. *The Bundle*. London: Eyre Methuen, 1979.

_____. *Lear*. London: Eyre Methuen, 1972.

_____. *Bingo*. London: Eyre Methuen, 1974.

_____. *The Fool and We Come to the River*. London: Eyre Methuen, 1976.

_____. *The Woman*. London: Eyre Methuen, 1979.

_____. *Bingo and The Sea*. New York: Hill and Wang, 1975.

_____. *The Bundle*. Chicago: Dramatic Publishing Co., 1978.

_____. *The Fool*. Chicago: Dramatic Publishing Co., 1977.

_____. *The Narrow Road to the Deep North*. London: Eyre Methuen, 1977.

_____. "Beating Barbarism." *Sunday Times*, 25 November 1973, p. 22.

_____. "On Brecht: A Letter to Peter Holland." *Theatre Quarterly*, 8, No. 30 (1978), 34-45.

_____. "Green Room: Us, Our Drama and the National Theatre." *Plays and Players* 26, No. 1 (1978).

Bowra, C.M. *Tradition and Design in the Iliad*. Westport, CT: Greenwood Press, 1977.

Bradley, A.C. *Shakespearean Tragedy*. Greenwich, CT: Fawcett, 1965.

Christenson, Sandra. "The Common Man in Bond's *Lear* and Shakespeare's *King Lear*," in *Edward Bond's Lear and Shakespeare's King Lear*. Wiesbaden: Steiner, 1974.

Cohn, Ruby. *Modern Shakespearean Offshoots*. Princeton: Princeton University Press, 1976.

_____. "The Fabulous Theatre of Edward Bond," in *Essays on Contemporary British Dramatists, 189-204*.

Coult, Tony. *The Plays of Edward Bond*. London: Eyre Methuen, 1977.

_____. "Creating What is Normal." *Plays and Players*, 23, No. 3 (1975), 9-13.

Dark, Gregory. "Production Casebook No. 5: Edward Bond's *Lear* at the Royal Court." *Theatre Quarterly* 2, No. 5 (1972), 20-31.

Dohmen, William F. "Wise Fools and Their Disciples in the Development of Edward Bond's Drama." *Kansas Quarterly*, 12, No. IV, 53-61.

Donahue, Delia. Edward Bond: A Study of His Plays. Rome: Bulzoni, 1979.

Donohue, Walter. "Edward Bond's 'The Fool' at the Royal Court Theatre," *Theatre Quarterly* 6, No. 21 (1976), 12-24.

Duncan, Joseph E. "The Child and the Old Man in the Plays of Edward Bond." *Modern Drama* 19, No. 1 (1976), 1-10.

Durbach, Errol. "Herod in the Welfare State: Kindermord in the Plays of Edward Bond." *Educational Theatre Journal* 27 (1975), 480-487.

Eagleton, Terry. *Marxism and Literary Criticism*. London: Eyre Methuen, 1976.

Edgar, David. "Ten Years of Political Theatre, 1968-78." *Theatre Quarterly* 8, No. 32 (1979), 25-33.

_____. "Theatre, Politics and the Working Class." *London Tribune*, 22 April 1977.

Esslin, Martin. "Nor Yet a 'Fool to Fame...'" *Theatre Quarterly* 6, No. 21 (1976), 39-44.

Fromm, Erich. *The Sane Society*. New York: Holt, Rinehard and Winston, 1955.

Gill, Peter. "Coming Fresh to 'The Fool.'" *Theatre Quarterly* 6, No. 21 (1976), 25-32.

Gorki, Maxim. "Art and Myth," in *Marxism and Art*. ed. Maynard Solomon. Detroit: Wayne State Press, 1981.

Hall, John. "Edward Bond." *The Guardian*, 29 September 1971, 10.

Hare, David. "A Lecture Given at King's College Cambridge," in *Licking Hitler*. London: Faber, 1978, 57-71.

_____. "From Portable Theatre to Joint Stock...via Shaftesbury Avenue," *Theatre Quarterly* 5, No. 20 (1975-76), 108-115.

Hay, Malcolm and Philip Roberts. *Edward Bond: A Companion to the Plays*. London: Theatre Quarterly Publications, 1978.

_____. *Bond: A Study of His Plays*. London: Eyre Methuen, 1980.

_____. "Edward Bond: Stages in a Life." *Observer*, 6 August 1978, 12-13.

Herbert, Hugh. "Edward Bond." *The Guardian*. 14 August 1974, 10.

Hobson, Harold. "*The Woman*: Plays in Performance." *Drama* (Autumn 1978), 43-45.

Holland, Peter. "Brecht, Bond, Gaskill and the Practice of Political Theatre." *Theatre Quarterly*, 8, No. 30 (1978), 24-33.

Hudson, Robert, Simon Trussler et al. "Drama and the Dialectics of Violence." *Theatre Quarterly* 2, No. 5 (1972), 4-14.

Hunt, Albert. "A Writer's Theatre." *New Society*, 11 December 1975, 606-607.

Innes, Christopher. "Edward Bond: From Rationalism to Rhapsody." *Canadian Theatre Review*, No. 23 (1979), 108-113.

Israel, Joachim. *Alienation: From Marx to Modern Sociology*. Boston: Alyyn and Bacon, 1971.

Itzen, Catherine. *Stages in the Revolution: Political Theatre in Britain Since 1968.* London: Eyre Methuen, 1980.

Jaspers, Karl. *Tragedy is Not Enough.* London: Victor Golanz, 1952.

Jones, Daniel. "Edward Bond's 'Rational Theatre'." *Theatre Journal*, 32, 505-517.

_____. *Edward Bond's Rational Theatre.* Unpublished Dissertation, Florida State University, 1978.

Lattimore, Richmond and Grene, David, eds. *Euripides III.* Chicago: University of Chicago Press, 1958.

Loney, Glenn. "Interview: The First Cycle." *Performing Arts Journal* 1, No. 2, 37-45.

Lukács, George. "The Sociology of Modern Drama," in *The Theory of the Modern Stage.* Ed. Eric Bentley. Trans. Lee Baxandall. Baltimore: Penguin Books, 1968.

Marx, Karl. *The Economic and Philosophic Manuscripts of 1844.* Ed. Dirk Sturik. Trans. Martin Milligan. New York: International Publishers, 1964.

Matherne, Beverly and Maiorana, Salvatore. "Interview with Edward Bond." *Kansas Quarterly* 12, IV, 63-72.

McCrindle, Joseph, ed. *Behind the Scenes.* New York: Hold Rinehart and Winston, 1971.

McGrath, John. "The Theory and Practice of Political Theatre." *Theatre Quarterly* 9, No. 35 (1979), 43-54.

_____. "The Year of the Cheviot." *Plays and Players.* February 1974, 24-30.

Mitchell, Juliet. *Woman's Estate.* New York: Vintage Books, 1973.

Murray, Gilbert. *Euripides and His Age.* London: Oxford University Press, 1965.

Nodleman, Perry. "Beyond Politics in Bond's 'Lear'." *Modern Drama*, 23 (1980), 269-276.

Ollman, Bertell. *Alienation: Marx's Conception of Man in Capitalist Society.* Cambridge: Cambridge University Press, 1976.

Oppel, Horst. "Success and Failure of Bond's Approach to Tragedy," in *Edward Bond's "Lear" and Shakespeare's "King Lear".* Weisbaden: Steiner, 1974.

Peter, John. "Edward Bond, Violence and Poetry." *Drama*, No. 118 (1975), 28-32.

Rademacher, Frances. "Violence and the Comic in the Plays of Edward Bond."
    Modern Drama, 24 (1981), 458-478.

Roberts, Philip. "The Search for Epic Drama: Edward Bond's Recent Work."
    Modern Drama, 23 (1980), 258-268.

_____. "Making Two Worlds One: The Plays of Edward Bond." *Critical
    Quarterly* 21, IV (1979), 75-84.

Roper, David. "Edward Bond in Conversation." *Gambit* 9, No. 36 (1980), 35-45.

Savona, George. "Edward Bond's *The Woman*." *Gambit* 36 (1980), 25-30.

Schacht, Richard. *Alienation*. Garden City, NY: Doubleday, 1970.

Scharine, Richard. *The Plays of Edward Bond*. Lewisburg, PA: Bucknell University Press, 1976.

Sewall, Richard. "The Tragic Form" in *Essays in Criticism*, 4 (1954), 345-358.

Smith, Leslie. "Edward Bond's 'Lear'." *Comparative Drama*, 13 (1979), 65-85.

Snell, Burno. *The Discovery of The Mind*. Cambridge: Harvard University
    Press, 1953.

Solomon, Maynard, ed. *Marxism and Art*. Detroit: Wayne State University
    Press, 1981.

Spenser, Jenny. "Edward Bond's Dramatic Strategies." in *Contemporary English
    Drama*, 119-137.

Stoll, Karl Heinz. "Interviews with Edward Bond and Arnold Wesker." *Twentieth Century Literature* 22, No. 4 (1976), 411-432.

Tener, Robert. "Edward Bond's Dialectic: Irony and Dramatic Metaphor." *Modern Drama*, 25 (1982), 423-434.

Trussler, Simon. *Edward Bond*. Harlow: Longman for the British Council, 1976.

Vasquez, Adolpho. *The Artist in Society*. New York: Monthly Review Press,
    1973.

Wardle, Irving. "A Discussion with Edward Bond." *Gambit* 5, No. 17 (1970),
    5-38.

Weil, Simone. *The Iliad as a Poem of Force*. Wallingford, CT: Pendle Hill,
    1968.

Willet, John, ed. *Brecht on Theatre*. New York: Hill and Wang, 1974.

Williams, Raymond. *Modern Tragedy*. Stanford: Stanford University Press,
    1966.

_____. *Culture and Society*. New York: Columbia University Press, 1983.

Worth, Katherine. *Revolutions in Modern English Drama*. London: G. Bell and Sons, 1973.

_____. "Edward Bond." *Essays on Contemporary British Dramatists*, 205-222.

Worthen, John. "Endings and Beginnings: Edward Bond on the Shock of Recognition." *Educational Theatre Journal*, 27 (1975), 466-479.